African Arguments

African Arguments is a series
today. Aimed at the growing
readers who want to know mֶ.ֶ. ֶ.ֶ..ֶ the African continent,
these books highlight many of the longer-term strategic
as well as immediate political issues. They will get to the
heart of why Africa is the way it is and how it is changing.
The books are scholarly but engaged, substantive as well as
topical.

Series editors

ALEX DE WAAL, Social Science Research Council
RICHARD DOWDEN, Executive Director, Royal African Society

Editorial board

EMMANUEL AKYEAMPONG, Harvard University
TIM ALLEN, London School of Economics and Political
Science
AKWE AMOSU, Open Society Institute
BREYTEN BREYTENBACH, Gorée Institute
CRAIG CALHOUN, Social Science Research Council
PETER DA COSTA, journalist and development specialist
WILLIAM GUMEDE, journalist and author
ALCINDA HONWANA, Open University
ABDUL MOHAMMED, InterAfrica Group
ROBERT MOLTENO, editor and publisher

Published by Zed Books and the IAI with the support of the following organizations:

International African Institute The International African Institute's principal aim is to promote scholarly understanding of Africa, notably its changing societies, cultures and languages. Founded in 1926 and based in London, it supports a range of seminars and publications including the journal *Africa*. <www.internationalafricaninstitute.org>

Royal African Society Now more than a hundred years old, the Royal African Society today is Britain's leading organization promoting Africa's cause. Through its journal, *African Affairs*, and by organizing meetings, discussions and other activities, the society strengthens links between Africa and Britain and encourages understanding of Africa and its relations with the rest of the world. <www.royalafrican society.org>

Social Science Research Council The Social Science Research Council brings much-needed expert knowledge to public issues. Founded in 1923 and based in New York, it brings together researchers, practitioners and policy-makers in every continent. <www.ssrc.org>

About the author

Theodore Trefon is a Congo expert specializing in the politics of state–society relations. He has devoted the past twenty-five years to Congo as a researcher, lecturer, author, project manager and consultant. Trefon's expertise derives from a career of analysis, participatory observation and extensive fieldwork. He is contributing editor to the *Review of African Political Economy*. Founding director of the Belgian Reference Centre for Expertise on Central Africa, he now heads the Contemporary History Section of the Belgian Royal Museum for Central Africa.

THEODORE TREFON

Congo masquerade

the political culture of aid inefficiency and reform failure

Zed Books
LONDON | NEW YORK

in association with

International African Institute
Royal African Society
Social Science Research Council

Congo masquerade: the political culture of aid inefficiency and reform failure was first published in association with the International African Institute, the Royal African Society and the Social Science Research Council in 2011 by Zed Books Ltd, 7 Cynthia Street, London N1 9JF, UK and Room 400, 175 Fifth Avenue, New York, NY 10010, USA

www.zedbooks.co.uk
www.internationalafricaninstitute.org
www.royalafricansociety.org
www.ssrc.org

Cover designed by Rogue Four Design
Cover photo by Per-Anders Pettersson/Getty Images
Set in OurType Arnhem and Futura Bold by Ewan Smith, London
Index: <ed.emery@thefreeuniversity.net>
Printed and bound in Great Britain by Mimeo Ltd, Huntingdon, Cambridgeshire PE296XX.

A catalogue record for this book is available from the British Library
US CIP data are available from the Library of Congress

ISBN   978 1 84813 837 7 hb
ISBN   978 1 84813 836 0 pb

Contents

Preface and acknowledgements

This book is about mismanagement, hypocrisy, powerlessness and sabotage. *Congo Masquerade* reveals the vacuity of reform logic and discourse. It is a study of aid inefficiency in one of the twenty-first century's major attempts at reconstructing a failed state in Africa. These attempts commenced at a time when state crisis was overwhelming: physical infrastructure was dilapidated, the macroeconomic situation was unmanageable and the population was debilitated by dictatorship, two regional wars and an exhausting political transition. These conditions have not made state reconstruction easy. They help explain why initiatives designed and implemented by Congo's international partners to reconstruct this huge and diverse country have, so far, been largely unsuccessful. International partners and Congolese authorities share responsibility in failing to bring about genuine political and institutional reform. The former have underestimated the complexities of political culture in Africa's third-largest territory; the latter, through ruse and strategy, deliberately hamper reform to stay in power.

Throughout much of the global South, it is increasingly obvious that development aid does not always develop. It does not always aid. Congo is fabulously rich but its people are abysmally poor. Congo is a land of broken promises. This book is designed to unmask the ineffectiveness of reform and development initiatives. The analysis reveals change without improvement. It presents a critical examination of why aid is not helping while offering a theoretical framework that inspires similar critiques in other state rebuilding contexts. *Congo Masquerade* can help engaged development experts,

NGO activists and academics improve the analytical tools needed to understand the pitfalls of reform initiatives.

As Congo is one of Africa's major development 'markets', the current situation needs to be reassessed with the kind of critical analysis that this book provides. The problems inherent to reform failure in Congo will not go away by themselves. This book makes explicit what many actors believe without having the courage or liberty to express their beliefs openly. *Congo Masquerade* is not an exercise in Congo bashing or Congo Schadenfreude. It is a critical and engaged assessment that seeks to fill an information gap by sounding an alarm. The objective is to shape dialogue about state-building challenges in this unsettling geography of imbalance. The spirit of the book is one of modesty and empathy because it raises fundamental questions about development and change. As the parable of the crocodile and the scorpion reveals (see page xx), we are merely groping for understanding with respect to the subtle intricacies of the reform process.

Masquerade may seem an insensitive term to associate with the Congolese social tragedy. But as revealed in the following chapters, it is a title that makes sense. Masquerade refers to situations of disguise and concealment where actors make a show of being what they are not, where they can be both themselves and their opposites. Hypocrisy and the art of the unsaid are key characteristics of masquerade. People wear masks and pretend not to recognize who is behind the masks surrounding them. But in fact everyone knows – or thinks they know – who the others really are. Masquerade is a process of jesting through dramatic situations or dealing with complex social relations with levity. It hides the true human nature of personal and political intrigue. Masquerade is largely synonymous with the hidden agendas of these protagonists, who have mutated into reform avatars. They are the forces that are contributing to the definition of Congo's still-uncertain process of becoming. Congo is indeed on the move. But do we know where it is headed? Unlike the masquerade of the

European Renaissance that contributed to comic reversal of social order, the 'Congo masquerade' of today appears far more tragic than carnivalesque.

Based on a political-anthropological approach, *Congo Masquerade* is constructed from a fairly exhaustive literature review, numerous field trips and experience of analysing state–society relations in Congo since the early 1980s. The Royal Museum for Central Africa's Contemporary History section possesses the world's largest documentation centre on Congo/Zaire. The historic depth and diversity of its collection, painstakingly maintained by Edwine Simons and Lore van de Broeck, have facilitated the writing of this book. While the Internet has changed researchers' access to information on the Congo by making reports, documents, press articles and forums accessible online, our library concentrates all kinds of published and unpublished material under a single roof with a user-friendly, numeric indexing system. The daily review of the Congolese press prepared by Guy De Boeck and the press articles archived on CongoForum (www.congoforum.be/fr/index. asp) have also been invaluable sources of information, as have the SYFIA Grands Lacs (www.syfia-grands-lacs.info), EURAC (www.eurac-network.org/web/) and IPIS (www.ipisresearch. be/?lang=en) websites and newsletters. The Congo Siasa blog (congosiasa.blogspot.com/) and excellent reports published by the International Crisis Group also merit special mention.

Chapter 1 explains why state-building is not working in the Congo. It looks at the different strategies and motivations of reform and state-building and argues that development aid does not always aid and does not always develop. The chapter makes some potentially controversial statements about reform as masquerade, such as the undesirable side effects of outside intervention, the strategies that Congolese actors design to manipulate their foreign partners and the crushing problem of competition between actors who rhetorically claim to be working towards a common goal but in fact distrust each other and sabotage reform initiatives.

Chapter 2 offers an overview of Congo's political economy, mainly since Joseph Kabila's ascension to the presidency in 2001. The objective here is not to present an exhaustive political chronology of events during this confused period of recent Congolese history but to embed the portrayal of events in the donor-driven reform and state-building agenda. Transition and electoral politics are analysed, relations with China are presented and the celebrations of fifty years of independence are depicted in such a way that the government's obsession with regime consolidation is revealed. A macroeconomic overview is also presented.

Empirical data and analysis supporting the main argument of the book are set forth in Chapter 3. Reform has not induced positive change and ordinary Congolese still live in dire poverty and insecurity. The topics included in this chapter are infrastructure, security, decentralization and industrial logging. The aim here is to provide cogent and convincing case studies without having the ambition of being exhaustive. The exercise could have included public health, mining, education, media or justice. Nonetheless, addressing all of these priorities would have made the book unwieldy and discussing the same patterns of reform failure would have resulted in unnecessary repetition.

Administrative reform is the subject of Chapter 4. It addresses the paradox of international partners having attempted to rebuild state and institutions without sufficiently thinking through the role of the Congolese civil servants who should be key intermediaries in reform initiatives. Evidence reveals that these very individuals have more vested interests in resisting reform than in fostering it. The chapter presents analysis of why the administration persists in the broader context of state failure and how it has mutated over time. It examines the highly complex, sometimes conflictual, sometimes accommodative relations that bind service users and service providers.

Culture matters. Chapter 5 tackles the complex question of

political culture. It addresses the strategies used by political insiders to dominate the voiceless hoi polloi. Local political culture is a difficult concept to harmonize with imported reform and development agendas but analysing it is important because it contributes to understanding Congo's reform challenges. The chapter looks at social stratification and political exclusion, manipulation of rumour, secrecy, (dis)information, repression, corruption and predation. These instruments of political culture are not new. They are stubbornly entrenched in Congo's troubled past. Revisiting these recurring patterns today is pertinent because it puts into perspective the ways in which political culture – and the culture of politics – influences the reform process and social change. Political culture helps account for the 'one step forward, two steps back' reform conundrum.

The two-part conclusion starts with an interpretation of the crocodile and scorpion parable, emphasizing the challenges of powerlessness, self-destruction, sacrifice and misunderstanding. It ends with a presentation of how encouraging social dynamics can put negative images of the Congo into perspective. Despite the failure of reform initiatives and ongoing political problems, agency is taking form thanks to the Congolese people's resiliency, creativity and capacity to overcome obstacles.

Many friends and colleagues have contributed to my understanding of the Congolese political and social landscape. Those that are particularly deserving of acknowledgement are Marie-France Cros, Filip De Boeck, Léon de Saint Moulin, Pierre Englebert, Bogumil Jewsiewicki, Noël Kabuyaya, Baudouin Michel, François Misser, Mutambwe Shango, Balthazar Ngoy, Pierre Petit, Roland Pourtier, Thierry Vircoulon and Koen Vlassenroot. Experts in government, donor and diplomatic positions have also helped me form opinions about the issues addressed in this book, but for reasons of political sensitivity it would be best that they remain anonymous. Edouard Bustin, Patrick Chabal, René Lemarchand, Jean-

Claude Willame and Crawford Young read and commented on all or parts of the manuscript and made valuable suggestions for improvements. The Royal Museum for Central Africa pays my salary to carry out research on the Congo. I consequently extend gratitude to director Guido Gryseels for institutional support and his respect for academic freedom. When I first contacted Zed Books about publishing *Congo Masquerade*, Ken Barlow was immediately supportive. I am grateful for his advice and professionalism. Amy Shifflette accompanied me in the research, writing, editing and production processes. She is warmly thanked for her positive energy and constant encouragement.

Timeline

1960 Independence from Belgium; Joseph Kasavubu elected president, Patrice Lumumba becomes prime minister; post-independence turmoil.

1961 Lumumba assassinated with the complicity of Belgium and the United States.

1960–63 Secession of mineral-rich Katanga province; first 'Congo crisis'.

1965 Joseph-Désiré Mobutu seizes power in a coup d'état.

1971 Mobutu renames the country Zaire.

1971–74 Nationalization of foreign investments; beginning of economic crisis.

1983–86 Financial and political crisis; World Bank imposes Structural Adjustment Programmes.

1990 Mobutu accepts the principle of multiparty politics and democratization.

1990–92 Political debate takes place in the framework of the National Sovereign Conference.

1991–96 Bankruptcy of private and public service; riots and looting sprees in Kinshasa; hyperinflation rate nears 1,000 per cent in 1994.

1996–97 War of liberation; Mobutu–Kabila transition.

1997 Zaire is renamed Democratic Republic of the Congo.

1997–99 No coherent economic policy; economy devoted to war effort.

1998–2002 Second Congo War; eleven African states involved.

1999 The United Nations Security Council establishes the United Nations Organization Mission in the Democratic Republic of the Congo (MONUC).

2001 Assassination of President Laurent-Désiré Kabila; Joseph Kabila becomes president.

2002 Joseph Kabila liberalizes economy and re-establishes

relations with IMF and World Bank; launch of major reform package.

2005 Eighty-four per cent of the country's 24.5 million registered voters approve the proposed constitution in a popular referendum.

2006 Joseph Kabila wins run-off presidential election in October; national legislative and provincial elections held.

2007 Post-election violence in Kinshasa and Bas-Congo.

2007–09 Continued insecurity in Kivus; no improvement in social conditions; economic growth below 3 per cent; political activity is dominated by regime consolidation.

2010 Congo celebrates fifty years of independence; major debt relief package agreed by World Bank and IMF; political assassinations continue with impunity; MONUC renamed United Nations Organization Stabilization Mission in the Democratic Republic of the Congo (MONUSCO).

2011 Presidential elections scheduled; electoral procedures modified by constitutional amendment.

Abbreviations

AMP	Alliance for the Presidential Majority
ANR	Agence nationale de reseignement
CENI	National Independent Electoral Commission
CNDP	Congrès national pour la defense du peuple
DRC	Democratic Republic of the Congo
EU	European Union
FDLR	Forces démocratiques de libération du Rwanda
GDP	gross domestic product
HIPC	Heavily Indebted Poor Countries
IMF	International Monetary Fund
MONUC	UN Organization Mission in the Democratic Republic of the Congo
NGO	non-governmental organization
OECD	Organization for Economic Cooperation and Development
PPRD	People's Party for Reconstruction and Democracy
UN	United Nations

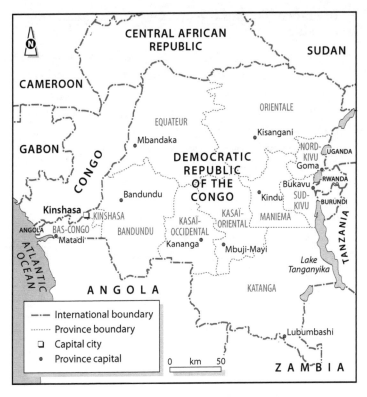

Map: Democratic Republic of the Congo

The crocodile and the scorpion: a Congolese parable

One afternoon in Kinshasa, a scorpion asked his friend the crocodile to help him cross the majestic Congo river. 'I have to cross over to Brazzaville but don't know how to swim. As you swim with such ease and elegance, let me climb on your back so we can leave without further ado.'

The crocodile replied: 'Dear scorpion, I know you and the reputation of your kind. Once we get to the middle of the river, you'll sting me and we'll both drown.'

'Why would I ever do such a thing?' asked the scorpion. 'If I sting you and you die, I'll drown with you.'

The crocodile thought for a moment and agreed to help the scorpion. 'Climb on; let's get moving before nightfall.'

They left the shore and headed for Brazzaville. As the lights of Kinshasa started to fade and their destination appeared on the horizon, the scorpion had a sudden urge and stung the valiant swimmer in the neck.

'Why did you do that?' asked the crocodile, who was nearing the end of his tether. 'I'm exhausted; we're never going to make it!'

Just before they both disappeared under the murky water, the scorpion whispered: 'That's the way it is. This is Congo. Don't try to understand.'

1 | Why state-building is not working in the Congo

The alchemy of state-building

Post-conflict Congo is a vast laboratory where a host of international partners are engaged in experimenting with different state-building alchemies. Security, poverty reduction, improved governance and rule of law, macroeconomic management and the physical rehabilitation of infrastructure are the principal objectives of state-building and reform. Yet, despite the significant amounts of international funding, the talent and strategic thinking of international experts and consultants, and even with the stated commitment of political leaders to embrace change, there is little tangible evidence of success. On the contrary, the evaluation of reform and reconstruction is resoundingly negative. International partners and Congolese authorities are handicapped by the constraints of their respective political systems. They share responsibility in failing to implement meaningful change. The overall picture of reform failure is the sum of a series of disconnected, uncoordinated and fragmented initiatives. Congo's bilateral and multilateral international partners have no master plan for reform. They do not share a common vision and often implement contradictory programmes. The aborted decentralization process, reform of the public service sector and absence of progress in security sector reform are examples. Congolese authorities obstruct reform efforts to maintain their positions of relative power. Many quite simply do not want change.

Ordinary Congolese also have somewhat dubious attitudes towards change. 'The devil we know is less terrifying than the one we don't know' is a commonly expressed sentiment. Reform policies superficially respond to symptoms without addressing the root causes of problems, such as the violence that emerges from deeply entrenched historical factors, social imbalances, institutional weakness, corruption and diverging perceptions of the need for change. Reform failure in the Congo reflects both the complicated power relations underpinning Congolese politics and society and the ambiguity that characterizes international idealism.

Poverty indicators (such as education, health, food security, condition of women and children) and vulnerability indicators (mainly physical security) are catastrophic. In some cases, they have even declined in reverse proportion to the initiatives designed, funded and implemented by Congo's international partners. Life expectancy at birth, in comparison to international standards, is extremely low (forty-five years). An official government report on the status of the Millennium Development Goals does not present a positive forecast. Of the thirteen goals and sub-goals, the country has 'no chance' of reaching targets for six goals and only a 'limited chance' of reaching the others (République démocratique du Congo 2010: 22). On the contrary, numerous development and humanitarian efforts have generated undesirable side effects. In the eastern provinces, most notably but not exclusively, significant amounts of euros and dollars spent on humanitarian assistance have been wasted. United Nations reports testify to this reality, as do humanitarian actors (Vircoulon 2010; Marriage 2006).

The Democratic Republic of the Congo (DRC) is systematically condemned by well-respected international monitoring sources. Notable examples are the Fund for Peace's Failed States Index, the World Bank's Doing Business in Africa annual assessment, the OECD's Human Development Indicators, and Transparency International's Corruption Perceptions Index. A telling statistic comes from the Food and Agricultural Organization (FAO): 50 per cent of the Congolese population is undernourished. A best-case scenario simulation suggested that 1960 development levels could be attainable by 2030, but only if growth rates remain strong until then (République démocratique du Congo 2006: 11, 27).

Political scientists have a fairly clear understanding of why states collapse and what constitutes state failure. The now classic criteria emphasize poor economic performance, political and institutional dysfunction, inability to guarantee security and law and order and unmet social expectations (Zartman 1995: 5–11). National governments in failed states, in other words, are unable to exercise legitimate control over their territory. Sophisticated concepts of state failure, however, do not diminish the trauma of hunger, disease, displacement and violence. This is the lived reality of millions of ordinary Africans. But political scientists and development experts do not know how to go about rebuilding failed states. The social challenge of reinventing and improving state–society relations is enormous because there are between forty and sixty failed or collapsed states; nearly one billion people live in them (Ghani and Lockhart 2008: 3).

Activists, academics and policy-makers agree that we are just starting to grasp the complexities and motivations – and paradoxically the disincentives – for state reconstruction. For some, the international community's interest in state-building is based on humanitarian, development and security concerns, as well as colonial guilt. This is reflected in the Western liberal discourse advocated in Europe and America. For others, China, for example, state-building is important for trade and commerce. There is also an emerging neoconservative agenda advocating that state-building is a fundamental security priority in the wake of 9/11 because failed states breed chaos, terrorism and conflict. This position is advocated by influential American policy-makers: 'Weak and failed states and the chaos they nurture will inevitably harm USA security and the global economy that provides the basis for American prosperity' (Eizenstat et al. 2005: 134). Another interpretation, a cynical one, focuses on the logic of deliberately reproducing state dysfunctionality and continued dependence on external aid. The aim is to sustain 'a series of failed states in which the international donor community will be able to dictate policy and exercise control long into the foreseeable future' (Hilary 2008). Congo/Zaire's long history of external intervention, pillaging

3

and resource wars gives some credence to this interpretation (Renton et al. 2007). Nonetheless, while some external actors may benefit from disarray in the Congo, most others pay a very high dysfunctionality price in terms of transactions costs and lost opportunities.

Aid inefficiency

Attempts to fit economic progress and development into a linear system, as proposed by liberal economists fifty years ago, proved unsuccessful. Their deterministic approach underestimated the hybrid and historically entrenched process of state formation in Africa, which, according to Bayart's much more nuanced analysis, 'has been an utterly haphazard and even confused process' (Bayart 2000: 246). Recent failures in international state-building efforts, be they in Afghanistan, Iraq, Somalia or Congo, prove that imported templates – one size fits all – do not always work. Standardized peace kits put together by United Nations agencies, the Bretton Woods institutions and the world's big donors are not automatic panaceas. A strong contingent of international experts will not necessarily guarantee success despite their sophisticated work plans and project-cycle management strategies. Templates tend to be strategically irrelevant, exported by donors and applied thoughtlessly to nations that differ in political, economic and cultural terms. The basic elements of these standardized peace kits include peacekeeping forces and logistical support, a new constitution, institution-building, governance programmes, transitional justice and media and civil society capacity-building (Vircoulon 2009a: 5). This approach has proved to be largely unsuccessful because state-building strategies tend to mask the importance of political culture and deeply entrenched sources of tension, hatred, distrust, ethnicity, violence and conflict. Conversely, external counsel has helped some African countries recover from destruction: Liberia, Sierra Leone, Uganda and Ghana, for example.

Aid inefficiency has been under scrutiny for many years. Two important books have stimulated fresh debate about how aid, in addition to not helping countries develop, in fact contributes to underdevelopment and despotism. David Easterly's *The White Man's Burden: Why the West's efforts to aid the rest have done so much ill and so little good* (2006) is a harsh critique of development strategies. Much of his analysis applies perfectly to Congo's present situation: there are sound policies but inadequate implementation strategies (ibid.: 6), aid experts desperately want 'to disbelieve the bad government explanation for poverty' (ibid.: 42), there is an insistence on the part of international financial institutions on 'transform[ing] bad government' instead of boycotting it (ibid.: 151), and the West engages in 'coddling awful gangsters who just call themselves a government' (ibid.: 153). Easterly also refers to the 'aspiration to a utopian blueprint' (ibid.: 367), which in Congo can be translated as the ambitious (but ambiguous) reform package designed by foreign partners who paradoxically never agreed upon a master plan.

In her immediately influential book, *Dead Aid*, Dambisa Moyo (2009) argued that development aid has sabotaged social capital, disrupted African financial initiatives and exacerbated corruption. Some of her observations based on the whole of the African continent have resonance in Congo: politics, not development priorities, dictate aid agendas; organizing elections is confused with fostering democracy; aid supports corrupt leaders instead of helping poor people; and civil society is undermined by making corrupt leaders accountable to donors and not to citizens. Although evidence from the Congo is compelling, Moyo's thesis is excessive because there are counter-examples where external assistance has correlated with some improved state function.

Development practitioners and aid experts themselves are now conceding defeat. A former World Bank spokesperson describes how 'some of the best economists in the world worked hard on Africa's problems, to little avail' (Calderisi 2006: 164). He condemns donors with the assertion: 'aid is both ineffective and demeaning, large amounts of it have simply been wasted. Even aid agencies have acknowledged repeatedly that there is greater pressure to commit money grandly than to spend it wisely' (ibid.: 167). A critique of recent European strategies emphasizes the gap between donor priorities and those of beneficiaries and the perverse effects that aid has by institutionalizing corruption and buttressing incumbents (Delcourt 2008: 8–9). The capacity of outside actors to bring about positive change is also questioned by OECD experts who claim that 'the processes of state-building are largely domestically driven and international state-building assistance has only a limited role to play' (OECD 2008: 13). An important strategic document for poverty reduction in the Congo is unequivocal in this view: Congo's dependency on foreign aid is a major obstacle to development (République démocratique du Congo 2006: 102). This is an argument that has been made for all of Africa. According to another 'anti-aid' expert, 'dependency on aid from foreign donors has undermined the development of the *basic institutions* needed to govern and the vital link of accountability between state and citizen' (Glennie 2008: 5–6). Like Moyo, he also argues that as a consequence of aid, some people have gained but many more have suffered (ibid.: 5) and 'the consensus that some would like us to think exists on aid and growth is an illusion' (ibid.: 83). Others have argued that state reconstruction efforts suffer because solutions tend to be perceived as being technical and not political (Anderson 2005). Humanitarian assistance is not immune to this kind of lucid evaluation. In her *Not Breaking the Rules, Not Playing the Game*, Zoë Marriage gives resonance to an example of understated hypocrisy: 'the optimism conveyed by the objectives of assistance is combined with an expectation of failure ...' (Marriage 2006: 7).

A recent trend in trying to reverse years of state-building failure and aid inefficiency entails focusing on governance issues and making aid recipient countries accountable to donors and their citizens (Joseph and Gillies 2009). While this trend makes sense in theory, there is little evidence to suggest that it could work in a context as complicated as that of DRC. The assessment is shared by former USAID deputy administrator Carol Lancaster: 'We are pretty sure the $1.6 billion in aid the United States has provided Democratic Republic of Congo since 1960 has failed to produce lasting positive development results, mainly because of the political context of corruption, incapacity, and conflict' (Lancaster 2009: 33). The rate of return on public development aid is clearly not commensurate with the amounts of money invested. It is more likely to be commensurate with its embeddedness in the political and cultural environment. As Englebert and Tull point out, trying to inculcate a culture of good governance and accountability does not sufficiently integrate an unforgiving state-building flaw. 'Whereas donors tend to see reconstruction as a new beginning after the crisis of failure, African elites more often see it as an ongoing competition for power and resources, facilitated by power-sharing agreements, increases in foreign aid, and lax international oversight' (2008: 121).

'Bringing the state back in' is part of the Congo reform roadmap, a discrete trend that emerged in the early years of Kabila rule when the West worked towards legitimizing him. The disdain for the Congo state felt by many international experts and project managers is only now, gradually, being reconsidered. The current implicit strategy is to rehabilitate the state at all costs, with or without Congolese involvement. The negative side effects of policies designed in the early 1990s, notably the 'delegitimization' of state power (Bongeli 2008: 119), are still being felt. When Mobutu outlived his usefulness to his Western backers after the collapse of the Soviet Union, international partners abruptly withdrew support for the Zairean state. They channelled their aid through non-governmental organizations (NGOs) and United Nations agencies. This gave birth to a project approach aimed at replacing a state considered to be corrupt and inefficient.

The project approach suffers from a number of problems. Congolese stakeholders are marginalized from the project-cycle decision-making process (notably identification and implementation) and qualified civil servants leave their administrations for better-paid work in internationally funded projects. This has translated into a series of projects that are not cost efficient, not viable and locally inappropriate. Project success continues to be evaluated in terms of amounts of money spent, rather

7

than in results. The need to spend donor money according to a project calendar ('absorption capacity' in project-cycle management jargon) is surrealist in DRC. This requirement, combined with an abysmal lack of pertinence, led one European Union expert to describe the Congo as a 'vast cemetery of projects'. Most people working in the development field have their own favourite story about a project gone wrong. Mine relates to an international conservation NGO that felt it had to do something to help villagers in the Salonga National Park in the middle of Congo's dense tropical forest. The NGO designed and constructed a cement and metal contraption to smoke fish. A year after it was built it was still unused. The absurdity results from the fact that those villagers have been smoking fish efficiently and sustainably for hundreds of years thanks to their own traditional know-how.

The project approach upon which much of the reform agenda is based necessitates working with competent Congolese. These focal points, resource people and project coordinators play an interesting but dubious role. While they often say 'the receiving hand is underneath the hand that gives', they transform what may appear as a situation of dependency into a situation of subtle pre-eminence. Donors, international governmental agencies and NGOs sometimes become dependent on these Congolese state-sponsored reform intermediaries who use their positions of relative power to address their own agendas. Projects continue to be sidetracked by those who feel vulnerable to the prospect of real reform or change. Even the most talented technical experts can become entangled in the Congo's Byzantine web of vested interests. The plan to integrate civil society stakeholders in implementing projects has also failed owing to the dominance of state actors. Indeed, civil society actors have been powerless to combat the Congo state's resistance to change. International partners recognize the limitations of the project approach and have thought about alternatives. One of these is direct budgetary support to state institutions, but this approach has also encountered operational problems.

Reform or masquerade?

In the arena of Congolese politics and international relations, masquerade is played out by local actors to obscure, dissimulate or camouflage their real objectives. International partners play the same game for similar reasons. Acting behind the mask of impunity enables reform protagonists to evade their official responsibilities. Because the system has institutionalized the multiplication of intermediaries, when things go wrong, it is never anyone's fault. Congolese authorities cunningly smother reform initiatives but without completely suffocating them. The twofold objective is to keep them alive (for funding, to maintain tolerable relations with foreign partners or to stay on board as part of a process). At the same time, they manoeuvre to slow down, block or sabotage reform. An astute Congo observer has labelled this strategy '"personally fruitful" stagnation' (Prunier 2009: 315). Congolese authorities have indeed been remarkably brilliant in manipulating an international system that contributes to foreign aid policy becoming ensnared in domestic politics. This subtlety did not escape Belgian foreign affairs minister Karel De Gucht when he made provocative comments in Kigali in October 2004 about the abysmal absence of leadership for the people in Congo, an opinion he continued to voice after becoming European Commission Commissioner for Humanitarian Aid. Mamadou Diouf (2002: 23) translates this subtlety as: 'fish cannot approve a budget for the purchase of fishhooks'. This calls into question the common assumption that international aid policy is based on rational and comprehensive decision-making strategies.

Were real reform to take place, many Congolese authorities, civil servants and NGO representatives would outgrow their usefulness. They would see their capacity to benefit from commissions and other forms of corruption diminish. Many international experts and consultants would also be out of work. They play the game of working for reform while making sure not to cut off the branch upon which they sit. In an analysis of emerging governance patterns and identity, Raeymaekers (2007) interpreted Congolese resistance to change through the paradox: 'everything

9

must change if we want to stay the same'. This is a fine example of *trompe l'oeil*. Trickery, mediation and rejection – key concepts in Bayart's analysis of extraversion – are thus applicable to the relations between Congolese and the West. Extraversion refers to the historically entrenched 'formalities of action which have constantly recurred in Africa's relations with the rest of the world throughout the 20th century' (Bayart 2000: 254–5). A history of colonial humiliation and dictatorship has helped Congolese learn to devise pragmatic modes of manipulation, communication, negotiation and accommodation to guarantee perpetually shifting patterns of domination.

The absence or sluggishness of reform is reminiscent of Mobutu's strategies of *ouverture politique* announced in 1990. This situation can be explained in part by the fact that the massive presence of international development efforts has taken the burden of responsibility off the Congolese government. Instead of being accountable to the people, the government reassigns the abstract notion of accountability to its international partners. The role of the United Nations peacekeeping mission is one concrete example of this form of reassignment. The same situation applies to the World Health Organization, which has assumed public health responsibilities, international environmental NGOs that struggle to manage Congo's rich natural heritage or churches that provide primary education. In the short term, political incumbents benefit from this substitution.

Many reform policies make sense at a theoretical level. Successful implementation, however, has not materialized, largely because of the absence of a reliable and motivated administrative structure. The balance between the utopia of what is desirable and the pragmatism of what is doable has not been struck. State structures that have been targeted for reform, including administrative services, often do not even exist or are so weak that reforming them is impossible. The new international partnership with Congo is tantamount to trying to stitch patches on a very tattered cloth. There is pomp and ceremony, conferences and workshops, signatures of official letters of intent and budget allocation – but little poverty reduction or increased well-being. For these reasons, it could be argued that the reform process is little more than masquerade. Many reform and reconstruction strategies, moreover, are condemned by the absence of maintenance budgets or follow-up policies. They are also condemned because foreign-driven initiatives rarely take into account local knowledge and know-how. According to James C. Scott (1998: 6): 'designed or planned social order is necessarily schematic; it always ignores essential features of any real, functioning social order'. Scott's analysis of 'the indispensable role of practical knowledge, informal processes, and improvisation in the face of unpredictability' (ibid.: 6) is a valuable lesson for reform experts working in Congo.

Masquerade also takes the form of the manipulation of anticipation: promises are made, team leaders are appointed, working groups are put together, committees are nominated and deadlines are set. Many international partners have fallen into the trap of their Congolese counterparts who pay lip-service to the need to reform but who in fact have designed clever strategies of resistance. Englebert and Tull's assessment of African political elites in general applies perfectly to those of Congo: '[They] share neither the diagnosis of failure nor the objectives set out by the foreign promoters of reconstruction policies. Instead, they seek to maximize the benefits accruing to them from these policies, as well as from ongoing political instability' (Englebert and Tull 2008: 110–11).

Strategies of resistance exist at the highest levels of the state, throughout the administrative structures and also at the project implementation level. They include splitting hairs on details while masking real issues, addressing peripheral – not central – issues and sidetracking (organizing a meeting while deliberately omitting to invite the main stakeholders, for example). Masquerade also takes the form of going through the motions by being physically present and visible instead of being productive or efficient. As in other societies, working and being at work are two distinct realities. Private sector investors have understood these subtleties and tend to be circumspect in their relations with the Congolese.

This explains why the enabling conditions the Bretton Woods institutions have tried so hard to establish have failed to attract international private capital, with the exception of investment in natural resource extraction.

Humanitarian aid delivery is a concrete example of the Congo masquerade. DRC remains one of the world's worst humanitarian crises. Violence, population displacement, rape of women, men and children, and the collapse of public health services prevail. Mortality rates are significantly higher than the sub-Saharan African average. Most deaths are due to easily preventable or curable conditions, such as malaria, diarrhoea, pneumonia, malnutrition and neonatal problems. These are all by-products of a collapsed healthcare system. The increasing role of NGOs (alongside UN agencies and bi- and multilateral agencies such as the EU's Office for the Coordination of Humanitarian Aid) is a notable trend in humanitarian aid over the past twenty years.

Humanitarian activities now include institutional support, combating the recruitment of child soldiers, aid coordination, non-governmental diplomacy and tracking the illegal exportation of natural resources. Despite what could potentially be a positive trend, humanitarian aid delivery suffers from serious handicaps, making it in many instances inefficient or counterproductive. These handicaps include: (i) excessive subcontracting whereby NGOs assume the role of donors, (ii) competition and rivalry between aid agencies, (iii) diverging perceptions of priorities and application methods between local and international partners, (iv) distribution of humanitarian aid for political purposes, (v) absence of reliable local partners and absorption capacity and (vi) serious logistical shortcomings. As in other sectors targeted for reform, the main obstacle to humanitarian aid delivery is the absence of a master plan based on consensus. Humanitarian aid can also have direct tragic consequences. In late 2009, thousands of Hutu civilians were attacked by Congolese national army troops when they sought healthcare offered by Doctors without Borders.[1] An estimated sixty-two civilians were killed in North Kivu areas controlled by rebel Hutus from the Forces démocratiques de libération du Rwanda (FDLR). Doctors without Borders said that their services were used as 'bait' for army forces to retaliate against civilians who were perceived as being FDLR sympathizers.

The United States and Britain participated in the masquerade through their long-standing and unconditional support for Congo's enemies during the worst episodes of the Congo wars. Rwanda's intervention in the Congo (and Uganda's to a lesser extent) and its impacts on security, the economy and social morale has been devastating. Washington and London were aware of the conditions leading up to the 1994 Rwanda genocide but chose not to act. Following the Rwanda genocide, President Clinton and Prime Minister Blair embraced Rwandan president Kagame as a peace-builder with a good governance discourse. They provided him with massive financial and diplomatic support, allowing him and his proxies to exploit people, land and minerals. Kagame justified the Rwandan presence in eastern DRC by arguing that Hutu forces operating in the Congo constituted a security threat. This security argument, although not exactly false, veiled the far more pragmatic explanation: Rwanda's unabashed plundering of Congo's gold, diamonds, coltan and other minerals. Despite the ostensible rapprochement between Kinshasa and Kigali and waning Anglo-American support for Kagame, ongoing Rwandan intervention continues to seriously undermine Congolese security and development.

Other examples of the Congo masquerade pertain to human rights and justice. Rule of law is poorly respected in DRC. It is one of the least free countries in the world, according to Freedom House.[2] For the UN's Committee on the Elimination of All Forms of Discrimination against Women, the promotion of women's human rights and gender equality is not seen as a priority. Freedom of expression is extremely limited. Journalists live under constant threat; intimidation is part of a strategy to censure the coverage of conflict and human rights violations.

Rule of law and improved human rights conditions are predicated on reform of the justice system. This was identified as one of the international community's main objectives in 2002. With less than 1 per cent of the budget devoted to justice, the sector has been forced to finance itself, like other administrative services. Justice consequently goes to the highest bidder. Congolese, like many other Africans, comment: 'Why pay a lawyer when I can buy a judge?' Reform actions during the transitional government include: (i) the abolition of the *Cour d'ordre militaire* (infamous for its death penalties), (ii) the creation of tribunals for business and commerce, (iii) a new military penal code, (iv) new statutes for magistrates, (v) corruption and sexual violence now being listed as penal infractions, and (vi) elaboration of prison reform. Since the ratification of the 2005 constitution, three broad reform avenues have been pursued: (i) restructuring of the entire legal system, (ii) setting up specialized legal departments (such as administrative and business tribunals, appellate courts, a Supreme Court, etc.), and (iii) drafting a new penal code. Cooperation between the international community and the Ministry of Justice is ongoing but progress remains slow owing to an absence of political will and financial resources. As many propositions go against deep-rooted practices, reform of the legal system can be summarized as change without improvement (Vircoulon 2009b).

Engineering reform and reconstruction in Congo is handicapped by a cluster of real obstacles and overwhelming challenges. The crisis is historically entrenched, politically entangled and socially complex. It is conceptually difficult to know where to start and financially impossible to address all the challenges at the same time. Some Congolese authorities and international experts argue that the most important priority is resolving the problems of security, putting reform of the army and police on the top of the list. Others argue that without tackling the problems of governance and high-level institutionalized corruption, all reform efforts will be meaningless. Other voices claim that a revolution in mentality is needed, making rehabilitation of the education system a prerequisite. Similar claims could be made for infrastructure, macroeconomic control or health. But there is no shared vision. There is no mutually acceptable master plan. On the contrary, there are too many plans, resulting in a blatant absence of harmonization among donors and Congolese authorities. The overall context of mistrust and suspicion and the tendency to address specific agendas before responding to common goals is both cause and consequence of this 'one step forward, two steps back' situation.

Competition is a major obstacle to reform and is rife at three different levels: between international partners themselves, between international partners and Congolese actors, and between Congolese authorities. The result is an unmanageable political context and a series of fragmented and frequently contradictory actions and strategies. Competition between international partners in the media sector is one example. According to Marie-Soleil Frère (2009a), it suffers from opposing ideologies and incompatible institutional and methodological formatting. Another example is the way that the Belgian Technical Cooperation and the United Nations Development Programme ended up at loggerheads with respect to their efforts to reform public service provision. In the security sector, there is the problem of 'parallel hierarchies' that contribute to competition and ineffectiveness (Pouligny 2006: 129). Moreover, as pointed out by Hoebeke et al. (2009), competition between donors stems from an even more complex, and tragic, set of conditions. They argue that it is part of a deliberately orchestrated strategy by the Congolese government to destabilize external coordination. Indeed, some high-ranking Congolese derive significant wealth and power by perpetuating low-intensity conflict in the eastern provinces. Their conclusion is that the systematic organization of insecurity is more profitable than the organization of security.

At the second level, the role and mandate of the UN peacekeeping mission is a good example of competition between foreign actors and the Congolese government. The UN considers that the security situation does not permit a withdrawal of forces. The government, for reasons of sovereignty and internal political consumption, say that they have the security situation under control. The decentralization debate is an example of the third level of competition. The central government has not moved ahead with decentralization for various reasons, including unwillingness to transfer financial resources and political control to some of the provinces wanting to move ahead to achieve greater autonomy. The fragile nature of the ruling government coalition, partisan politicking and power-seeking strategies also testify to the internecine competition at the national level. Diverging views can also result in some high-profile political bickering over relatively trivial issues. The government was mobilized in September 2010, for example, by incompatible opinions about *Tintin in the Congo*. For the minister of culture the comic book is a masterpiece; for other high-ranking officials, it represents Africans as naive and primitive and should be banned.[3]

Jockeying for power and competition exists within the international community's big institutions too. At the European Commission level, for instance, foreign policy is divided between different external relations clusters, each of which has Congo desks or experts. Discussions on Congo between experts from the EuropeAid Cooperation Office, the Directorate-General for Development or the European Commission Humanitarian Aid and Civil Protection Office testify to fragmentation and institutional haggling. A similar situation exists within United Nations structures. In a cogent analysis of UN function and dysfunction in the Congo, Autessere reports that:

> The UN valued MONUC's electoral and political affairs sections more highly than the mission's humanitarian, human rights, or civil affairs departments, as evidenced by the number of people deployed in each unit and their ranks. In the field, the head of the political affairs or the electoral section was often the number two, just below the head of office, whereas the heads of the humanitarian, human rights, or civil affairs sections were much lower in the hierarchy. (Autessere 2010: 218)

Still another level of competition is the one that exists between high-ranking Congolese authorities and their administrative services. This is a common hierarchical problem worldwide and exists in Western democracies as well as in failed states. Nonetheless, the nature of state crisis in Congo, notably with respect to human resource management, exacerbates this problem. Absenteeism, privatization of the public work space, inadequate office material, recruitment strategies and the lack of satisfactory salaries are a few examples of factors that weaken the chain of command. Even if authorities appropriate the logic of reform, they do not always have the means to incite their staff to implement directives.

Perverse side effects also result from individual actions carried out without comprehensive feasibility studies or understanding of local culture and practices. For example, an international medical NGO provided mosquito nets to a village in the Upemba region of Katanga which has a high rate of malaria-induced child mortality in lakeside villages. But this laudable action created another problem. Fishermen used the mosquito nets as fishing nets and, given their extremely fine gauge, not only were fish removed from the lake but all other forms of micro-fauna and micro-flora too. The lake gradually became covered with a black scum; villagers lost their sources of livelihood and food supply. It took a Belgian priest two years to get the villagers, who believed they had been cursed, to understand what had happened before the lake was able to regenerate.

Engineering reform and reconstruction is also handicapped by an equally impressive number of socially constructed obstacles. Extending deadlines, the perpetual redefinition of priorities and negotiating the means to implement them are hallmarks of the Congo masquerade. Many attitudes and behaviours that govern patron–client and social relationships in Congo escape Western development logic. Congolese construct their identities according to social and cultural patterns that are not necessarily conducive to state-building priorities, which again helps explain their failure. The importance of witchcraft and the invisible world is the most remarkable example (De Boeck 2004a). There is also a wide gap between Western and Congolese perceptions of well-being. Politics in Congo, moreover, is ethnic. Nonetheless, for reasons of pseudo-political correctness, or the inability of development experts to comprehend it, this powerful reality is rarely explicitly

17

woven into the complex web of reform. Extreme secrecy, discreet but constant surveillance, wielding social capital in deal-making, reliance on the extended family, perceptions of personal honour and occupying spaces of real or perceived power with little concern for achieving results are further examples. The manipulation of rumour is another contrivance that often escapes Western development logic. It can be used for political advantage or can serve as a powerful levelling mechanism (White 2004). These attitudes and behaviours help Congolese mask reality and hide the truth in their dealings with reform or development experts. While feigning a simulacrum of dependency, Congolese influence and often control their foreign partners.

2 | The political economy of broken promises

Mobutu to Kabila père *and* fils

The origins of crisis in Congo's political economy take root in the patrimonial system put in place by King Leopold II. The territory was his personal property from 1885 until 1908 when it became a Belgian colony until independence in 1960. Mobutu Sese Seko also exploited the Congo as if it were his personal property. Because of Cold War politics, the West supported him unconditionally despite severe human rights abuses. When the Soviet Union collapsed, Mobutu outlived his strategic usefulness and was forced to accept democratic transition.

In 1992, the National Sovereign Conference was organized, encompassing over two thousand representatives from various political parties. The Conference gave itself a legislative mandate and elected Archbishop Laurent Monsengwo as chairman, along with Union for Democracy and Social Progress (UDPS) leader Etienne Tshisekedi as prime minister. Mobutu continued to dominate the political landscape and created a rival government with its own prime minister. The ensuing stalemate resulted in the compromise merger of the two governments into the High Council of Republic-Parliament of Transition in 1994, with Mobutu as head of state and Kengo Wa Dondo as prime minister. Although presidential and legislative elections were scheduled repeatedly over the next two years, they never took place. The end of Mobutu coincided with Laurent-Désiré Kabila's capture of power and broader turmoil in the Great Lakes region.

Between 800,000 and 1 million Tutsis and moderate Hutus were massacred in Rwanda in 1994. At least 1.2 million refugees then poured into the Kivus, including 100,000 *Interahamwe* (Hutu militias from Rwanda and Burundi). In late 1996, Banyamulenge (members of the Tutsi community indigenous to South Kivu), supported by Rwanda, started a rebellion. This facilitated the creation of the Alliance des forces démocratiques pour la libération du Congo-Zaire (AFDL) in 1996. The first Congo war, or 'the war of liberation', was relatively short lived (October 1996 until May 1997). It was then that Laurent-Désiré Kabila gained control of Kinshasa and proclaimed himself president. In May 1998 Kabila broke with his former backers and organized new power networks based on his ethnic group, the Baluba. This led to the formation of the Rassemblement congolais pour la démocratie (RCD), which was the main rebel group fighting to overthrow Kabila and the AFDL.

Laurent-Désiré Kabila was president from May 1997 until his assassination in January 2001. But being president is one thing; managing the nation is something else. Dictatorship is the term most often associated with Mobutu. Disintegration best summarizes the Laurent-Désiré Kabila years. His cabinet and advisers had little or no experience in government. He demonstrated little ability to manage the problems of the country and alienated his allies, who rapidly turned against him. As the economy plunged deeper into crisis, he relied on shady business deals that mortgaged the country's mining assets. Pillaging of natural resources was widespread, economic growth was negative, official exports fell, inflation skyrocketed and the value of the Congolese franc plummeted. It was a period of 'financial improvisation' (Prunier 2009: 237). When Kabila was assassinated by a bodyguard (who was immediately liquidated himself), his regime controlled less than 50 per cent of the national territory.

In Byzantine fashion, Joseph Kabila became president after his father's assassination and was subsequently designated president of the transitional government in 2003. Many Congolese believe that L.-D. Kabila was not his biological father but rather his stepfather. Joseph Kabila, at this turning point in the history of Congo, 'was caught up between the demands of an international community for which his father incarnated everything that was wrong with African politics and those of a close "palace guard" that had decided to carry on with those very policies that had so alienated the dead man from the rest of the world' (ibid.: 257). Joseph was once commander of the infamous army of child soldiers (*kadogos*). Upon assuming the presidency, he broke with his father's economic policies, largely because of the necessity to re-establish relations with donors. In need of legitimacy, Joseph Kabila immediately sought the support of Belgium, France, the USA and Bretton Woods institutions. This was the start of a new Congolese fiasco because these partners fell into the trap of legitimizing what would rapidly become a corrupt and inefficient political machine. It was a period described by René Lemarchand as being one of 'tunnel at the end of light' (2009: 249).

Fragile peace and transition

After months of bitter negotiation between former belligerents and rival Congolese factions, the Inter-Congolese Dialogue was resumed, resulting in the setting up of a transitional government on 30 June 2003. Its foundation had been laid in the December 2002 Pretoria Agreement (Bouvier with Bomboko 2004). This phase was perceived as a fragile dénouement to the very bloody Congo wars of 1996/97 and 1998–2002 (Lemarchand 2009; Prunier 2009; Reyntjens 2009; Turner 2007). Because of the number of actors involved, former US Secretary of State Madeleine Albright described the 'unresolved turmoil' in DRC as 'Africa's first world war'.[1] It was in the context of this international concern that a United Nations peacekeeping force was approved by the Security Council in November 1999, mainly to put an end to hostilities in the eastern provinces, as outlined in the July 1999 Lusaka Agreement. This agreement sought to achieve the departure of foreign armies and militias (Weiss and Carayannis 2004; Willame 2002). Nonetheless, ten years later, this objective has not been achieved. European Union initiatives, such as Operation Artemis (2003) or the Quick Reaction Force, have not been more effective (Willame 2010: 122–3). A further series of negotiations, the Sun City Dialogue, held in South Africa in February 2001, also failed because the terms outlined in the Lusaka Agreement were not respected. The Lusaka

Agreement has been described as a 'charade' (Prunier 2009: 223), largely because it was 'completely unfit for dealing with the reality on the ground' (ibid.: 225). There is some consistency between this situation and research that shows that 'civil wars ended by negotiated settlement are more likely to recur than those ending in victory by one side' (Toft 2010: 7).

A transitional government was set up in July 2003. Its main objectives were to (i) reunite, pacify and re-establish governmental authority throughout the Congolese territory, (ii) foster national reconciliation, (iii) reform security forces by integrating rival factions, (iv) organize elections and (v) set up new political institutions. Implementation of these objectives, however, was made difficult, and in some cases impossible, because of the awkward power-sharing arrangements of the transitional government – and particularly the 1+4 formula of one president and four vice-presidents (Muzong 2007: 8). Prominent politico-military leaders such as President Kabila, Vice-President Jean-Pierre Bemba and Vice-President Azarias Ruberwa, although members of the same transitional government, did not share views on these objectives. They bitterly competed for turf, most notably concerning the presidential elections of 2006. The problem was inherent in a larger, more dubious flaw regarding the logic of the transition process, which sought '... to buy peace by giving all signatories to the deal lucrative positions, an accommodation that came at the cost of continued impunity for human rights abuses and corruption and left intact patronage networks that permeate the state and army' (International Crisis Group 2007: ii). Impunity has also been described as being the 'glue' of the peace process (Stearns 2007: 202). Impunity and the absence of accountability significantly continue to hamper the implementation of reforms.

After the ratification of the Third Republic constitution in December 2005, presidential elections were held in 2006. An unexpected 25 million Congolese registered to vote. The international community paid approximately $500 million to cover the cost of the electoral process under the supervision of the Independent Electoral Commission (StrategiCo. 2007: 22). As Kabila was viewed as the 'likely and preferred winner of the elections' (International Crisis Group 2007: 2), he received strong support from the Kinshasa-based CIAT (Comité international d'accompagnement de la Transition). The CIAT was a parallel executive body heavily involved in elaborating strategies and policies relating to political, economic and security priorities. It played a major role in giving direction to institution-building policy during the transition period. *Sauver le pouvoir* (support the incumbent power) was the expression many Congolese, especially from Kinshasa and the diaspora, used to describe what was commonly perceived as the hidden agenda of the CIAT. Another example of the Kabila legitimization strategy included a pledge of $3.9 billion at a donors' consultative group meeting in Paris for project financing for the government action programme 2004–06 in December 2003 (Clément 2004: 45). This was part of a much larger financial package to support the transition and post-election phases of nearly $15 billion between 2001 and 2007. This foreign support earned Kabila the reputation of being 'the candidate of the White man' (Reyntjens 2009: 272). The consultancy firm Stevens & Schriefer, which was part of the George W. Bush for President media team, orchestrated the Kabila electoral campaign.

The replacement of state functions by international partners is not a phenomenon restricted to the transition or post-election periods. It has been a gradual process accompanying state failure. In 1991 Prime Minister Kengo wa Dondo asked the European Commission to take on the role of National Authorizing Officer (*Ordonnateur national*). This entitled the Commission to assume part of the functions of the government to implement its projects, while managing funds directly from Brussels. In 2001, the government of Joseph Kabila asked the European Commission to continue acting as National Authorizing Officer for the implementation of the National Indicative Programme of the 8th European Development Fund. This situation, whereby the Kinshasa-based political elite and big donors compromised on the role of the Congo state as an 'absentee landlord' (Kobia 2002: 434), unique in the history of EU–Africa-Caribbean-Pacific (ACP) relations, lasted until 2007.

It is a good example of the process of transforming the country into an international protectorate, sometimes referred to as the 'neotrusteeship' approach (Fearon and Laitin 2004). The Kabila regime at this juncture was put under tutelage; its sovereignty was circumscribed and controlled by international partners (de Villers 2009: 227).

Under the aegis of Congo's international partners, who invested heavily in legitimizing Joseph Kabila (without, however, fully assessing the longer-term implications), the security and political context improved slightly. Progress was faltering, but sufficient to identify priority reform sectors. Very quickly after being parachuted into the presidential office, the young Kabila revisited his father's economic policies, renewing with the International Monetary Fund and the World Bank. The month after he took office, these institutions sent a 'relatively large' multisector mission to Kinshasa, including monetary, financial, exchange rate and fiscal experts (Clément 2004: 13). Given the absence of reliable national-level quantitative macroeconomic data, one can wonder on what basis these experts prepared their strategic plans.

One can also wonder about the legitimacy of the Bank and IMF involvement given the failure of previous efforts at reforms. The Structural Adjustment Programmes of the 1980s sought to establish economic stability by containing budget deficits, narrowing the gap between official and black market exchange rates, improving public sector management, redefining trade policies and providing incentives for private sector investment. Structural Adjustment did not help. Over half of the national budget was devoted to debt service. The economic situation worsened, severe poverty became rampant and unemployment escalated. The development of the informal economy – which enables the vast majority of Congolese to survive today – can be explained by Mobutu's nationalization policies of the mid-1970s. More specifically, however, it is a direct repercussion of a failed Structural Adjustment Programme. It could nevertheless be acknowledged that not all IMF initiatives in the Congo have backfired: a reform programme launched in 1967 successfully stabilized the currency for several years.

Based on experience in other post-conflict countries such as Liberia and Sierra Leone that resulted in some success, these institutions coached, nudged and assisted the government in designing a patchwork of reform initiatives. These included ambitious macroeconomic measures, facilitating and attracting private investors (Investment Code of February 2002), reform of the natural resource sector (Mining Code of July 2002 and Forestry Code of August 2002), preparation for the restructuring of public enterprises and efforts aimed at fighting corruption in the public sector (Code of Ethics and Good Conduct of November 2002) (Gons 2004).

Election euphoria and political hangover

As incumbent with access to state finances, media coverage and security, Kabila dominated the electoral landscape. He established a coalition of disparate regional and ethnic-based groupings, the Alliance for the Presidential Majority (AMP). Clever strategic partnerships were secured with Nzanga Mobutu, the former president's son, Antoine Gizenga, who headed the Unified Lumumbist Party (PALU), and Kyungu wa Kumwanza of the National Union of Federalists of Congo (UNAFEC). Kabila also benefited from a weak and fragmented opposition. Etienne Tshisekedi, long-time Mobutu opponent and head of Union pour la démocratie et le progrès social (UDPS), made poor strategic decisions. His worst miscalculation was ordering his followers to boycott the entire electoral process. The Congolese Rally for Democracy (RCD) was widely unpopular because of its close links with Rwanda and succeeded in marginalizing itself, notably in the Kivus, because of its extreme violence and brutality. Azarias Ruberwa's weak leadership led to the desertion of some key RCD officers. Jean-Pierre Bemba's Movement for the Liberation of Congo (MLC) also saw the desertion of some prominent allies, such as Olivier Kamitatu, José Endundo and Alexis Thambwe, who were to receive key ministerial positions in the Kabila government. Kamitatu and Endundo subsequently committed an act of *lèse majesté* in May 2010 by attempting to set up a new political group, the Liberal

25

and Patriot Centre (CLP), but were quickly brought back into the AMP fold (Le Potentiel 2010).

The long and complicated presidential election process resulted in a tightly contested Kabila victory; he scored 58 per cent, ahead of Bemba's 42 per cent. Kabila won firmly in the east. Bemba was the favourite in the politically volatile capital. As Kabila expected to obtain the necessary majority in the first round of voting, he considered the need for a run-off as an unwelcome electoral message, especially given his poor results in Kinshasa. But the results of the parliamentary elections, which did not follow the east–west cleavage, proved somewhat more favourable for the presidential coalition. The Alliance for the Presidential Majority garnered absolute majorities in the National Assembly (338 seats out of 500) and in the Senate (55 out of 108). The president's own party, the People's Party for Reconstruction and Democracy (PPRD), won the most seats.

Despite the gradual emergence of independent public media in most African countries, government control over state media is politically entrenched. Regimes continue to have direct influence on the role media play during elections. New electoral regulations stipulate that all candidates and parties should benefit from equal access to public media, but in practice the imbalance in favour of incumbents is striking. During a specific time slot during campaigning, the Congolese broadcasting regulation body observed that during the first round of the presidential elections in 2006, national television (Radio et télévision nationale congolaise) devoted nearly two hours to President Joseph Kabila. The other thirty-two candidates received only twenty-two minutes in total. For the election run-off, national television newscasts devoted nearly two hours to Kabila and ten minutes to Bemba (Frère 2009b: 189).

Well-respected NGOs such as Human Rights Watch and the International Crisis Group severely condemned human rights abuses in the post-election period: 'in the two years following elections, there have been disturbing signs that Congo's democratic transition is not only fragile, but that the newly elected government is brutally restricting democratic space. The government of President Joseph Kabila has used violence and intimidation to eliminate its political opponents' (Human Rights Watch 2008: 6). In an effort to hobble Bemba, for example, overzealous troops loyal to Kabila clashed with Bemba militiamen in Kinshasa in March 2007. Casualty reports range between 330 and 500 victims (Stearns 2007: 207). Hundreds of deaths were also confirmed following another bout of state-run intimidation in the Bas-Congo province in February 2007 and March 2008. Kabila's special forces used excessive violence against the Bundu Dia Kongo (BDK) political-religious group. BDK was seen as a threat to Kabila because it promoted greater autonomy in the strategically important and wealthy province, and because it had achieved electoral popularity. During the election, BDK had supported Bemba.

Organizing the elections and getting Congolese to vote given the overwhelming logistical problems were major accomplishments. Nonetheless, voting did not increase the democratic space and it seems that democracy was sacrificed on the altar of elections. The Western push to get Congolese to the ballot box was aptly described by Autesserre as 'elections fetishism' (2010: 218). Elections in fragile states are considered to be successful if they do not result in violence. According to this scenario, then, the elections in Congo failed. Democratization, as it was when Mobutu opened up politics in 1990, was a strictly controlled, top-down exercise. These new episodes of violence proved to the international community, and specifically to the architects of the electoral process, that popular consensus would not necessarily emerge from successfully engineered elections.

Democratization can be tested by elections but elections do not necessarily contribute to democratization. Even when elections are free and fair, they do not always result in the rule of law. Fighting and bloodshed served to reframe questions about the motivation, timing, approach and local pertinence for political and institutional change. They provoke the question of how much space there is in Congo for political pluralism, and also showed that the very concept of Western-style democracy is artificial to many Congolese (some even define democracy as 'a perfect dictatorship'). In the spirit of traditional authority models, they perceive consensus as being preferable to majority dictatorship. The search for consensus also helps account for the often long and intricate negotiation strategies that are omnipresent at all levels of state–society relations in DRC.

Foreign support of the electoral process in Congo lends credibility to an argument made by Chabal and Daloz (2006: 29): 'present transitions are unable to change the nature of politics in Africa. The holding of regular multiparty elections, which is usually equated with "democratization", has come about largely because of outside pressure, but the realities on the ground are that, more often than not, it is democracy that has been adapted to the logic and rigors of clientelism and not, as so often proclaimed, the reverse.' Englebert puts this in similar terms: 'More often than not, democratically elected elites have failed to implement meaningful change and have returned to the clientelistic and authoritarian politics of yore' (2009: 2). A comparable point has been made by Gillies and Joseph (2009: 13–14): 'The achievement of locally determined development goals, and their sustainability, depends ultimately on the nature and interplay of domestic forces, especially local socio-political dynamics. These can neither be created nor replaced by foreign actors.' But the nexus between elections and democracy is difficult to dismiss outright. Although African elections can be fraught with problems, as lessons from Côte d'Ivoire, Kenya and Nigeria reveal, they remain part of the democratic project. It has been argued that there are correlations between broad state performance indicators and the existence of democratic or semi-democratic institutions (Bratton and van de Walle 1997).

In an analysis of reform failure in the justice sector, Vircoulon makes a similar point. He argues that governance reforms often constitute well-designed public policies supported by foreign experts but their real impact is insignificant because they do not take into account the realities of 'petty politics' and implementation constraints (Vircoulon 2009b: 100). One of the most astute observers of his own society relates at an anecdotal level that Congolese have rebaptized the concept of 'democratic' transition into 'demonic' transition because of what is popularly perceived as unwelcome Western interference in Congolese affairs (Yoka 2009: 250).

Voting in Congo created false hopes. Electoral promises have not been transformed into concrete results. People had high expectations of the president's ambitious development programme (*cinq chantiers*) but have now come to see it as a political slogan and not a commitment for action.[2] Some central areas of Kinshasa have benefited from road and infrastructure improvements but the *cinq chantiers* programme has not extended into the provinces. Infrastructure, health and education, water and electricity, housing and employment are the five pillars of the programme. In lieu of access to clean drinking water, for example, Kinshasa residents say they 'drink air'. Ordinary Congolese sardonically say that the struggle to survive is their personal *sixième chantier*, their sixth development objective. They consider lack of progress in making democratic institutions work as a deliberate political strategy aimed at maintaining incumbency to the detriment of social and economic priorities.

On 30 December 2006, Antoine Gizenga was appointed prime minister by Joseph Kabila and became head of government in February 2007. In March 2007, World Bank president Paul Wolfowitz and European Union Commissioner for Development Louis Michel travelled together to Kinshasa to support the new government. They identified governance and state-building as the new priorities that these strategic partner institutions would promote. The elderly Gizenga formed a seemingly inclusive government with a cumbersome sixty ministers and vice-ministers. His objective was to try to satisfy the major stakeholders in the broad presidential alliance. Gizenga's mandate was complicated by what the International Crisis Group analysed as an '... absence of cohesion, coherence and a minimum common vision [...] The governing coalition of over 30 parties, which formed behind Kabila to gain powers and share spoils, is broad and unruly' (International Crisis

29

Group 2007: 9). Prunier's analysis of the governing coalition is equally unflattering: '... the AMP is an incoherent gaggle. It is not a "government" in the proper sense of the word, but rather a coagulation of groups operating out of completely mercenary interests ...' (Prunier 2009: 315). This context resulted in government paralysis that served the headliners in the Kabila camp. 'With the government mostly impotent, they continue to run the country from the presidency' (ibid.: 315).

The real work of law-making that the two chambers of parliament could be expected to perform was handicapped at the outset by the plethora of small parties and loose coalitions: seventy parties in the National Assembly and twenty-six in the Senate. Vital Kamerhe, an erstwhile Kabila ally, was speaker of the National Assembly and was able to maintain some consistency in voting patterns until he fell out with the president. Parliament, under Kamerhe's helm, was critical of the Congo–China deal and the 'secret' agreement made between Kabila and Rwandan president Kagame. This agreement allowed for the incursion of Rwandan troops into Congo in 2009 without informing parliament. Kamerhe, who was increasingly perceived as a presidential rival, was ousted and replaced by PPRD hardliner Evariste Boshab. Parliamentarians were allegedly bribed to facilitate the removal of Kamerhe (International Crisis Group 2010: 9). This was corroborated by US ambassador Garvelink, who wrote in an official diplomatic cable that $200,000 changed hands.[3] Control of the Senate has proved more difficult for President Kabila. Kengo wa Dondo, former Mobutu ally and Kabila opponent, was elected to head it and thus assume from a constitutional perspective the second-most important political position in the country.

The paralysis that characterized the prime ministership of Gizenga continues to bedevil the government of his successor and protégé Adolph Muzito (PALU), who was sworn in as prime minister in October 2008. Also dominated by members of the People's Party for Reconstruction and Democracy, his government does not govern. Decisions are made by the president's inner circle: the balance between government, Parliament and the judiciary is 'practically nonexistent' (ibid.: 1). Instead of working towards the priorities of implementing the reforms analysed in Chapter 3, politics in the Congo is dominated by efforts to consolidate presidential power, in large part because of the 2011 elections. The modification of electoral procedures that were validated by constitutional amendment in January 2011 is an example. Changing the presidential voting system from two rounds to one is a clear advantage for the incumbent.

Setting up the National Independent Electoral Commission (CENI) is another example of how the president has manoeuvred to silence potential critics. The Independent Electoral Commission (CEI) played an important role in the post-transition electoral process. Its functions included voter registration, maintaining voters' rolls, implementing voting operations, vote counting and announcing results. To organize the 2011 elections, the CEI was replaced by a new body, the National Independent Electoral Commission (which took four years to set up). The composition of the new body sparked debate in parliament owing to the absence of civil society representatives. The Senate proposed a board with nine members (four from the ruling majority, three from the opposition and two from civil society) but the National Assembly rejected the proposition. The exclusion of civil society is perceived as a tactic of the ruling majority aimed at sabotaging the neutrality of the electoral process. A Congolese civil society organization, Nouvelle société civile congolaise, consequently rebaptized the National Independent Electoral Commission as the National Non Independent Electoral Commission.[4]

A general characteristic of repressive regimes is the absence of a broad cadre of political actors able to form opinions and stimulate political debate. It is striking that a country as populous as Congo should have so few national political figures. Just like Mobutu, who had his *barons du regime*, and Kabila *père* with his inner circle of Katangais, Joseph Kabila relies on a few select advisers. Unlike his father, who had multiple special advisers for the same issues, Joseph appears to have concentrated power in the hands of key allies. As potential political rivals emerge, they are either called to order (as when Olivier Kamitatu, José Endundo, Mbusa Nyamwisi and Modeste Bahati sought to create a splinter party in May 2010) or sidelined (removal of Vital Kamerhe from the presidency of the National Assembly in April 2009). A Congolese proverb describes this levelling process and testifies to its embeddedness in political culture: when a tree stands out in the forest, the wind blows it down.

The *éminence grise* of the Kabila presidency is Augustin Katumba Mwanke. Although he does not hold any official position in the Kabila cabinet, he heads the Alliance for the Presidential Majority (AMP). His voice in economic matters is taken seriously. Already close to Kabila *père*, this Katangais was behind the Congo–China deal and is very influential in facilitating relations between the Kinshasa political elite and the mining sector. Adolphe Lumanu from Western Kasai province, minister of the interior and security, is another Kabila faithful. His appointment as minister followed a term as Kabila's head of cabinet. Lumanu had the task of announcing the suspension of John Numbi following the assassination of Floribert Chebeya in June 2010. Numbi had been Kabila's security boss since 2007 and also held the title of General Police Inspector. This native of North Katanga was not sacked but suspended and replaced by the Tutsi general Charles Bisengimana. Very close to the president, Numbi was the architect of some delicate special operations, such as the joint Rwanda–Congo military operation in North Kivu and the bloody repression of the Bundu dia Kongo political religious movement in Bas-Congo. Kabila also succeeded in placing a faithful ally as president of the National Assembly to replace the recalcitrant Vital Kamerhe. Evariste Boshab, from Western Kasai province, has proved his loyalty to Kabila as head of the president's party, the People's Party for Reconstruction and Democracy (PPRD). Given the composition of the National Assembly with its various political groupings, including loud opposition voices, Boshab's role requires finesse and a lot of political savvy. Strong support from the all-powerful Katumba Mwanke facilitates his role as institutional deal broker. Another representative of the Katanga establishment is Jean-Claude Masangu Mulongo. Governor of the Central Bank of Congo since 1997, he is one of the country's leading economists. First appointed by Laurent-Désiré Kabila, he was confirmed by Joseph. Known as the father of the Congolese franc, Masangu played an important role in reconnecting the Congo with the Bretton Woods institutions. Katanga governor Moïse Katumbi is a rather unique actor. Super-rich businessman turned politician, Katumbi combines tough business acumen with a populist approach to governing the mineral-rich province. Respected and liked by the Katangese, it appears that he will continue to support Kabila in 2011 – for the sake of his commercial empire. Kabila's twin sister Jeannette seems to have a strong influence over the president, especially with respect to commercial affairs. Israeli businessman Dan Gettler, active in the mining sector and generous contributor to Kabila's 2006 campaign, is another personality that merits special mention.

Beyond this small group of faithfuls, Kabila has had to accommodate himself with some other influential political figures. He maintains a tenuous relationship with Prime Minister Adolph Muzito from Bandundu province, who also heads the Unified Lumumbist Party (PALU). As PALU has strong support in much of the western part of Congo, Kabila needs to maintain good relations with him for electoral reasons. The second-most important person in the official Congolese state apparatus is a Zairean 'dinosaur' – a leading figure under Mobutu – and no friend of the president. Léon Kengo wa Dondo was a surprise choice as Senate president, confirming the reality that only the unpredictable is predictable in Congo. A particularly cagey politician on the Congolese landscape is Olivier Kamitatu. Erstwhile ally of Jean-Pierre Bemba, Kamitatu was president of the National Assembly during the transition and entered the government with an important portfolio as minister of planning. The major absent force on the political landscape is Bemba. Although a close rival during the presidential elections of 2006, the head of the emasculated opposition Mouvement pour la libération du Congo is on trial in The Hague for crimes against humanity. A former Kabila ally- (ex-head of the PPRD) cum-rival is

Vital Kamerhe. Widely popular in his home region of South Kivu, where Kabila won the vast majority of votes in 2006, Kamerhe is a political force to reckon with before the next presidential vote.

The Chinese honeymoon

One of the most significant developments throughout Africa in the twenty-first century is the increasing presence of China. The country has strategically shifted away from supporting radical ideologies as it did around the world a generation ago. Chinese radicalism inspired Congolese rebel leader Pierre Mulele in the 1960s. China has now positioned itself as a major economic investor that respects political neutrality. Beijing has a long-term strategy that combines claims to natural resources, aid and investment. China promotes its deals as being win-win based on the principle of mutual benefit. Its deal-making in Africa has nonetheless sparked the antagonism of Africa's traditional partners in the West. They see it as a threat to their commercial interests and in contradiction to their strategy of aid being conditional upon democratization and good governance. African leaders perceive that China has succeeded in taking hundreds of millions of Chinese out of poverty while fifty years of post-colonial aid have not helped the continent develop (Brautigan 2009). China's presence has made it clear that the West no longer has the monopoly over Africa's development agenda (Kragelund 2009). According to the Carnegie Endowment for International Peace and other sources, such as Transparency International, corruption poses a serious threat to China's economic development and political stability and it has a spillover effect in the foreign countries where it is investing (Pei 2007). In a corrupt, non-transparent country like Congo, this partnership has all the potential to become a very shady marriage of convenience.

Chinese relations with Congo date to the 1970s and have to be understood in the context of Mobutu's strategy of diversifying sources of foreign aid. It was after his symbolic visit to China in 1973 that he banned Western-style dress and introduced the Mao-inspired *abacost* (*à bas le costume*) jacket. Subsequent

34

to the visit, China built an 80,000-seat stadium in Kinshasa, a monumental pagoda at Mobutu's extensive agricultural complex in N'sele and the parliament building (*le Palais du peuple*). China also constructed an agricultural tool factory and supported the National Rice Programme. When Laurent-Désiré Kabila became president, he developed an anti-imperialism and anti-Western discourse. This opened new opportunities for exchanges with China. Chinese companies invested in mobile phone services and infrastructure, hospitals and health clinics, and Congolese students received scholarships to study in China. Congolese businessmen started commuting between Congo and China, importing containers full of cheap products 'Made in China'. Today, China is the number-one recipient of Congolese exports and continues to intensify its activities. It is now the major foreign commercial partner to track in Congo.

In September 2007, China pledged a massive two-phase financial package amounting to approximately $10 billion. In the first phase, $6.5 billion was earmarked for infrastructure and development. More than 3,500 kilometres of roads were to be built and upgraded and the same number of kilometres of railroads rehabilitated. Kinshasa was slated for a major facelift with a complete overhaul of the emblematic Boulevard du 30 juin, finished just in time for the commemoration ceremonies marking fifty years of independence. There were also projects to build thirty-two hospitals and 145 clinics, two universities and five thousand houses (Marysse and Geenen 2009: 379). The package also includes two hydroelectric dams, the rehabilitation of two airports and plans for a 1-million-hectare palm oil plantation. Military cooperation and arms deals are also on the agenda (La Libre Belgique 2010). Chinese companies are undertaking the work, which is funded by a loan from the Chinese Export-Import Bank.

Reimbursement of the loan is guaranteed by a complicated joint venture arrangement that is essentially a barter deal. It is complicated because it combines trade, investment, funding and development aid. It is a montage that contrasts sharply with Western-style logic, which separates development aid from private investments. In exchange for the loan, China receives rights to mine 8 million tons of copper, 200,000 tons of cobalt and 372 tons of gold. The second phase of the package is a $3.2 billion loan for the modernization of mining infrastructure. Guaranteed by the Congolese government, this would excuse China from paying taxes and duties for a thirty-year period. No other country or international financial institution has come close to initiating such a massive project in such a short period of time. It is noteworthy in the context of Congolese politics that what is commonly referred to as the 'deal of the century' did not require parliamentary approval. As it is a commercial agreement (not an agreement between two states) the constitution requires the government to inform the National Assembly but does not require its ratification (de Villers 2009: 431). This proves that important decisions are taken at the top, outside of participatory frameworks. Even representatives from key ministries such as Finance, Economy or Budget were not actively involved in the negotiations, despite the implications it could have for the country. As a consequence of this lack of transparency, little is known about the fundamental terms of the deal, including information about the pricing of minerals, what specific infrastructure projects are planned (and at what cost) and, finally, at what rate profits are to be taxed.

The 'deal of the century' did not exactly unfold as originally planned. Convincing criticisms were voiced because of its numerous flaws. Congolese opponents perceived the deal as a sell-out of the country's natural resources, suspecting it was a ruse to veil the political elite's scheme to grab money at the expense of ordinary Congolese – while allowing China to reap disproportionate profits. One Congolese lawyer investigating the deal emphasized that it would not contribute to development: '$6 billion in infrastructure is not development. Schools with desks are not going to educate our population. A road is not going to develop this country. Schools require a school system, and they need teachers. In this climate, roads last only ten years without maintenance, and the Congo has no capacity in this regard' (French 2010).

Europe and the United States disapproved because of the

absence of the conditionalities that have become part and parcel of Western development aid (such as respect for human rights, good governance, the environment and due diligence). The IMF and the World Bank firmly opposed it because they saw it as a source of new debt that the Congo would not be able to absorb, re-creating a spiral of poverty induced by indebtedness. Because certain commitments were made prior to carrying out relevant feasibility studies, there were also concerns that the mining concessions in the deal would not be able to cover the costs of infrastructure investment. As the government was negotiating with the IMF and the World Bank for relief from debt incurred under Mobutu, it gave in to pressure, resulting in a revision in 2009. The controversial infrastructure-for-minerals deal was consequently downsized, putting a $3 billion infrastructure phase on hold and removing the government's guarantee on the mining project. This revision provides further evidence that Congolese sovereignty is still in a situation of neo-trusteeship. The reduction from $6 billion to $3 billion for infrastructure imposed by Washington could be interpreted as making sense from a debt sustainability perspective. Nonetheless, the reduction deprives Congo of funds for basic development. Again, this reveals the multiple logics and agendas that motivate the different state-building protagonists.

While the revision of the contract was a relative setback for China, it was a more serious disappointment for Kabila. Chinese infrastructure work provided badly needed evidence to the Congolese people that the president was able to get something done concerning development, especially given the delays in respecting his nationwide reconstruction programme. Even though ordinary people would in fact have been responsible for the longer-term costs of the work because of the unequal terms of the barter agreement, it provided good visibility for the incumbent government. While the Chinese were adamant about not revising the contract, they had to accept the requirements imposed on the government by Washington. Like Congo's more traditional partners, the Chinese learned that work in Congo does not always move along as planned. In a similar vein, a Chinese technician laying down optic fibre between Matadi and Kinshasa declared that it was easier to dynamite through stone than to deal with Congolese customs officials (Le Soir 2009).

A tarnished golden anniversary

Fifty years of independence! June 30 2010 was an emblematic turning point for most Congolese. Rich and poor, old and young, Congolese living inside Congo and abroad all had an emotional rendezvous with the half-century date separating them from their colonial past. For Belgians, too, the date was characterized by nostalgia, emotion and stocktaking. In Brussels, the famous Manneken Pis statue was dressed in the colours of the Congolese flag. For President Kabila, the ceremonies constituted a boost to his image, thanks to the presence of high-ranking international dignitaries. This is a good example of how clever the Congolese authorities are at instrumentalizing foreign partners – and in this case an important historic event. It was a blessing for the Kabila government when the Belgian royal palace announced that King Albert II and Queen Paola would accept the president's invitation. Some Flemish politicians objected. Critics expressed the sentiment that Belgium was better at celebrating anniversaries than thinking proactively. The royal visit was supposedly conditional on real improvements with respect to governance, human rights and the fight against corruption. The Belgian monarch, a descendant of Leopold II, participated in the Congo masquerade by agreeing to go to Kinshasa despite the clear absence of improvements in these key areas. UN secretary-general Ban Ki-moon, President Paul Kagame of Rwanda and Yoweri Museveni of Uganda as well as more than thirty other high-ranking international dignitaries also attended the festivities. The vast majority of Congolese wondered what they would be eating that evening. The overall context for them was one of insecurity and misery (Cros 2010a). The international and Congolese press were largely critical of the ostentatious expenditures surrounding the celebrations, given the dire poverty of the population. This criticism was echoed by Belgian prime minister Yves Leterme, who participated in the ceremonies in Kinshasa (Laporte 2010). The sentiment of frustration was exacerbated when it was reported that President Kabila offered a set of diamond jewellery to Queen Paola. Although the royal palace acknowledged the gift, even characterizing it as 'a monumental mistake committed by the Congolese',[5] the Congolese ambassador to Brussels publicly denied that the luxury gift was offered by the president, specifying that it came from the First Lady (La Dernière Heure 2010).

The internal and international image of the Kabila government suffered a serious blow in June 2010, shortly before the celebrations, when a well-respected human rights activist, Floribert Chebeya, was found murdered. The UN, the USA, the EU, France and fifty-five international NGOs immediately put pressure on the government to investigate what was widely perceived as a political assassination. They have called for a non-partisan and transparent investigation, but Congolese civil society actors are sceptical about the likelihood of learning the truth. Kabila said that the investigation would be carried out by the Congolese, with Dutch assistance, even though the country does not have the appropriate forensic experts and laboratories that such an investigation would require. The head of police, John Numbi, with whom Chebeya was supposed to have had a meeting the day he was killed, was suspended as a first move taken by President Kabila.

Chebeya campaigned against King Albert II participating in the fiftieth anniversary celebrations; he organized a sit-in in front of parliament to protest about the removal of Vital Kamerhe; he was finalizing a complaint to be lodged at the International Penal Court against the perpetrators of the Bas-Congo Bundu dia Kongo massacres; he was critical of the government's foot-dragging in setting up the CENI; he was investigating the murder of a woman by the name of Aimée Kabila, who claimed to be the president's sister. Chebeya had clearly become a thorn in the side of the government. Just as the circumstances of the assassination of Laurent-Désiré Kabila remain unclear, unravelling who murdered Chebeya may never be possible. While it is likely that the government played a role, questions will remain unanswered about who exactly was involved. Accusations have been made against the president, his inner circle and overzealous police. It was even rumoured that the opposition could have been responsible to discredit Kabila. In Congo, things are not always what they may seem to be – which is a recurring characteristic of masquerade.

Congolese human rights groups wanted to organize Chebeya's funeral services on 30 June to coincide with the Independence Day celebrations. This would have been an embarrassment to President Kabila and his honoured guests. Chebeya's family (who subsequently moved to Canada) decided to hold the funeral on 26 June. They claimed that more frequent than usual electricity cuts at the hospital morgue resulted in the putrefaction of the corpse, which needed to be buried before the 30th. Chebeya's family attributed the electricity cuts to Kabila's entourage (Rogeau 2010). A few months after the Chebeya fiasco, Armand Tungulu Mundiandambu died under mysterious circumstances in the notorious Tshatshi military camp while in the custody of Kabila's Republican Guard. Tungulu threw a stone at the president's motorcade in Kinshasa on 29 September and was arrested on the spot. Two days later, he 'committed suicide' by hanging himself with 'a thread from his pillow'. This affair sparked demonstrations in Paris and Brussels, where outraged opposition activists, knowing that inmates at Camp Tshatshi do not receive pillows, concluded that the Republican Guard are not very good liars.

Macroeconomic overview

DRC was the second-most industrialized country in Africa at independence. It is one of the poorest countries in the world today. Economic decline started as a result of predatory economic practices, poor governance and insufficient investment under Mobutu. Nationalizations in the early 1970s and the expropriation of commercial enterprises by the state and their allocation to supporters of Mobutu caused a drastic decline in investment and output. By the late 1980s the Zairean economy had collapsed. Protracted conflict had a devastating impact on the economy:

infrastructure suffered considerable damage, many institutions were destroyed, assets were lost and investment came to a halt. The economy contracted by an annual average of 5.2 per cent between 1996 and 2001. Per capita GDP fell steadily from $380 in 1960 to $240 in 1990 and further to $85 in 2000. Since then, progress has been poor: per capita GDP was estimated at $96 in 2009 (Mushobekwa 2009).

Congo is often referred to as a 'geological scandal'. It is the world's largest producer of cobalt ore and a major producer of copper and industrial diamonds. It has cadmium, cassiterite, gold, silver, tantalum, tin, zinc, etc. The bombs that destroyed Nagasaki and Hiroshima were made from Congolese uranium. Rare metals found in mobile phones, computers and other everyday electronic items are mined, often illegally, in the eastern provinces, where plunder continues to fund conflict.[6] Small-scale informal mining has serious social and environmental repercussions. Mining revenues fuelled the Belgian colonial enterprise. President Mobutu exploited the sector for personal enrichment and political survival. Laurent-Désiré Kabila used it to fund his war efforts. According to best-case estimates, the gross production value of the mining sector for the period 2008 to 2016 will range between $2.0 billion and $2.7 billion annually (Andrews et al. 2008: 6).

Supported by the World Bank, which sought to formalize the industrial mining sector and put it at the centre of Congo's macroeconomic development programme, the government launched a series of reforms. The most important one was the 2002 Mining Code, which offered attractive tax incentives to investors. While a series of accompanying measures followed, aimed at making the Code workable, they have not significantly altered rent-seeking practices by political elites. These initiatives coincided with the restructuring and privatization of the Gécamines (Société générale des carrières et des mines), the big state-run mining conglomerate. The result was described as a major pillaging operation carried out by high-level Congolese authorities in collusion with their new private partners (Mazalto 2009: 177).

A review of sixty-one mining deals between 2006 and 2009 was carried out, in principle, to clarify the terms and agreements of concessions awarded by Kabila *père*. Forty-three contracts were approved, seventeen rejected and decision is pending on another.[7] The Joseph Kabila government, however, did not seriously commit to improved investment transparency through the review process: 'companies were obliged to negotiate under the table as well as across it' during the review years (Wallis 2010). Freeport McMoRan, Lundin, First Quantum Minerals and Katanga Mining Ltd are among the major actors, but they are under increasing competition from new Chinese, Israeli, South Korean, Brazilian and Indian players. The review process entailed minute scrutiny, negotiating, questioning and renegotiating but did not result in a safer, risk-free investment environment that could have encouraged the shift from access to a concession to exploitation. On the contrary, it served the short-term interests of political elites. As the political system thrives on negotiation, it tries to sustain and multiply the transaction process, constantly adding new phases, steps and procedures. Decisions don't matter; prolonging the negotiation process does. The mining review is a good illustration of how negotiation is both the expression and the tool of patrimonial governance.

Western partners have designed strategies to improve the management of the mining sector. The World Bank and the British government, for example, launched Promines (Growth with Governance in the Mineral Sector Project for Congo).[8] Its aim is to strengthen the capacity of key institutions to manage the sector, improve the conditions for increased investments and revenues from mining and help increase the socio-economic benefits. President Obama signed an important bill in July 2010 aimed at reducing corruption and conflict from mineral-rich poor countries. The Dodd-Frank Wall Street Reform and Consumer Protection Act requires oil, gas and mining companies registered with the US Securities and Exchange Commission to publicly disclose their tax and revenue payments to governments around the world.[9] It also requires companies to disclose information about the origins of tin ore, coltan, wolframite and gold. This initiative could be a constraint to corruption if realistic verification mechanisms are put in place and if there is sufficient pressure to make sure legislation is respected. For the time being, however, Congo's vast mineral potential has not produced dividends for ordinary Congolese. It does, however, allow political elites to consolidate their power.

There has been some macroeconomic recovery since the accession of Joseph Kabila to power in 2001 and the end of the civil war. But increased production of revenues has not resulted in socially equitable distribution. The government, supported by the Bretton Woods institutions, implemented a programme of macroeconomic reforms. These have aimed at establishing economic stability, poverty reduction, directing resources towards the rehabilitation of infrastructure and reforming the civil service and banking sectors. Exchange controls put in place by Kabila *père* were terminated, the currency floats freely and parastatals have been obliged to enter into joint ventures with private sector companies. Fiscal discipline and transparency have improved slightly, and monetary growth is more controlled. Rent-seeking practices by the government continue, though appear increasingly constrained by international supervision, such as the European FLEGT Action Plan,[10] the Independent Observatory established to review applications for forest concessions[11] and the Extractive Industries Transparency Initiative (EITI).[12] New domestic legislation designed to protect investment and property rights is being elaborated but investment security has never been worse, despite promises made by the government, according to one well-informed source (Risques Internationaux 2010).

Implementation of the economic reform programme was relatively satisfactory until about mid-2005. It deteriorated during the pre-election period, but recovered again in early 2007 following the appointment of the Muzito government. Reforms facilitated an inflow of foreign assistance and spurred private investments, especially in the trade, transport, construction and mining sectors. Roughly $2.7 billion in new investments has been registered by the government since early 2003. This reflects private sector

43

interest in the country's immense natural resources. Investment has been focused on rapid-return activities, mostly in Kinshasa and Katanga, in high-growth sectors such as telecommunications, agro-business, construction and natural resource extraction.

The investment climate is DRC is uninviting. The World Bank's 'Doing Business 2011' report places DRC at the bottom of the ranking: 175 out of 183.[13] In 2011, the World Bank's private investment arm, the International Finance Corporation, put a moratorium on new activities in DRC until further notice after the government cancelled a large investment project led by Canada's First Quantum Minerals Ltd. The case is now before an international arbitration court in Paris (Kavanagh 2010). The *Wall Street Journal*'s Economic Freedom Index puts it in 172nd position out of 179 for 2010.[14] Corruption, arbitrary taxation and bureaucracy and the absence of investment-enabling conditions explain these poor ratings. To prepare for the 2011 elections, improving the investment climate is a stated objective of the Muzito government, but again discourse has not been transformed into objectively verifiable results.

Table 2.1 presents some data on the macroeconomic situation. Statistics and figures, however, have to be considered with reserve because DRC has an extremely poor record of collecting and analysing macroeconomic data. When browsing through World Bank and IMF, Organisation for Economic Co-operation and Development and United Nations tables about worldwide data on development and economics, there are many blanks in the DRC column or row. Even in the best of circumstances, experts working in the Congolese National Office of Statistics (INS) would not be able to do their work properly if data from throughout the national territory were not collected and transferred regularly and systematically. But Congo remains a country of disinformation because, in addition to political constraints, administrations are poorly equipped and poorly trained. Staff are underpaid and consequently suffer from a lack of motivation.

Most economic activity in DRC takes place outside the official economy. The phenomenon emerged in the crisis years of the

TABLE 2.1 Selected macroeconomic data (2008–10)

	2008	2009	2010*
Growth of GDP (%)	6.2	2.7	6.0
Inflation, end of period (%)	27.6	24.8	15.0
Underlying fiscal balance (cash basis) as % of GDP	0.8	0.2	-0.5
Overall fiscal balance (cash basis, incl. grants) as % of GDP	−1.2	−4.2	−9.3
Non-government investment as % of GDP	19.2	15.0	16.1
Gross official reserves (end of period, in millions of $)	78	269	416
Gross official reserves (weeks of non-aid-related imports)	1.0	3.0	3.6
Scheduled debt service (in millions of USD)	291.4	257.3	154.5
Foreign exchange FC/$1	639	677	900

Note: * Estimates   *Source:* Mushobekwa (2009)

late 1970s and early 1980s but took on current proportions in the early 1990s. The informal economy includes activities that are unrecorded and, to varying degrees, illegal or illegitimate. They are cleverly designed at all levels of society to avoid administrative control and taxation. They include small-scale street vending, large-scale trading and manufacturing, cross-border smuggling, and schemes intended to avoid payment of taxes on legal production. Smuggling, hustling, pilfering and other unofficial activities also characterize the informal economy of DRC. The informal economy enables people to survive, but not to develop. It provides access to goods and services unavailable in the collapsed official economy, compensating for deficiencies in infrastructure and services, transportation, distribution networks and access to credit. The magnitude of the informal economy far exceeds official recorded economic activity.

The 2010 state budget was promulgated by President Kabila

on 25 January 2010 with nearly a month of delay. A first version was unacceptable to the president because it would have given a significant percentage to parliamentarians in the form of perks and salaries, depriving the government of resources needed to respect its commitment to make 2010 a year for social well-being – which is Joseph Kabila's political discourse in the run-up to elections. He was also particularly attentive to the budget as it was at the centre of discussions with the World Bank and the IMF in the context of debt restructuring – notably in the framework of the Heavily Indebted Poor Countries (HIPC) initiative. This resulted in relief for a large portion of the country's external debt in July 2010. This year's budget gives priority to the salaries of police, military, civil servants and teachers. The 2010 national budget amounts to $6.2 billion – or around that of a mid-sized European city. The DRC budget is seventy-seven times smaller than that of France, which has around the same population. More than half comes from international donors, mainly in the form of development aid. Bilateral and multilateral donors provide funding to Congolese ministries as institutional support, which indirectly reinforces the small national budget. Although insignificant considering the country's natural resources, the budget has admittedly been increasing steadily since 2001. The budget issue is politically interesting for two reasons: one, it reveals once again that political culture initiated under Mobutu persists and respects the logic of 'help yourself first', and two, it is a concrete indicator of World Bank control of the national government, especially concerning financial decisions.

Elaborated with the IMF, the Congolese authorities' programme for the period mid-2009 until mid-2012 includes the following targets: (i) average real GDP growth of 5.5 per cent; (ii) end-period inflation rate of 9 per cent by 2012; (iii) gross reserves equivalent to ten weeks of non-aid imports by 2012; and (iv) the external current account deficit (including grants) limited to an average of 25 per cent of GDP (Mushobekwa 2009). Given the extreme vulnerability of the Congolese economy to external shocks (such as global financial downturns, commodity price volatility and exchange rate fluctuations) there is little certainty that these targets will be met.

Until July 2010, DRC was in debt distress with an external debt stock of about $13.1 billion. It is particularly noteworthy that this amount resulted from borrowings of $3.5 billion between 1967 and 1975 (Marysse et al. 2010: 44). The remainder was interest, debt servicing and penalties on arrears. During the Cold War years the West tolerated the corrupt system put in place by the Mobutu dictatorship and encouraged heavy borrowing to recycle petrodollars (Zacharie 2009). This situation could be considered as odious debt, a legal theory stating that national debt incurred by a regime for purposes that do not serve the best interests of the nation should not be enforceable. In the twilight of the Mobutu period and the presidency of Kabila *père*, the country was off track with respect to its creditors – meaning that debt payments were suspended. By the end of 2008, debt services amounted to one quarter of total government expenditures and publicly contracted or guaranteed external debt was an estimated 93 per cent of GDP, 150 per cent of exports and 502 per cent of government revenue, excluding foreign aid. Given the large shares of the official bilateral and commercial debt in the total debt stock (59 and 33 per cent, respectively), reaching the Decision Point under the enhanced HIPC initiative took place only in July 2003.

The government received a magnificent fifty-year independence anniversary present from the international financial community. In July 2010, just days after the celebrations, DRC reached the Completion Point under the HIPC initiative. This means that $12.3 billion of Congo's $13.1 billion debt stock was forgiven. Strict criteria were required, including publishing information on partnerships with mining companies, improving the foreign investment environment, improving fiscal transparency and approving a law governing procurement practices. Implementing the Strategic Plan for Growth and Poverty Alleviation (DSCRP) was also a condition that emphasized pro-poor spending.

There is no question that granting Congo Completion Point status was based much more on political considerations than macroeconomic results. There was political motivation to stabilize Kabila in view of the upcoming 2011 presidential elections. Given the Bretton Woods institutions' commitment to the debt relief process, it would have been self-defeating to delay the decision. If Congo was perceived to have failed, then the IMF and the World Bank would have failed too. Washington was also under pressure to grant Completion Point status out of concern that, by not doing so, it would have lost bargaining power with the Congolese about revising the Congo–China deal.

Debt relief also means that, overnight, the government reaped a virtual windfall of $300,000 per year that it ostensibly plans on injecting into high-profile social actions for electoral purposes. In this context, the government reiterated pledges to make primary education free of charge. While the immediate reaction to the announcement was enthusiastic, parents, teachers and school administrators have subsequently voiced their scepticism because funds have not been injected into the school system. The predicable lack of follow-up makes the declaration meaningless. An even more troubling absurdity is that President Kabila is eligible to tap into funds made available in the poverty reduction mechanisms approved by international donors. He can use this option to build up an electoral war chest to pay for things like the four-by-four vehicles promised to all of the country's public university professors.

3 | A patchwork of unrealistic reforms

Territory versus state

Henry Morton Stanley immediately recognized that the Congo would be worthless without a railway. King Leopold II gave the undertaking his undivided attention. Later, setting up and maintaining a transportation network was a relatively successful accomplishment of colonial rule. Mobutu understood that he inherited from the Belgians a territory that needed to be transformed into a nation. At the policy declaration level it seems that these lessons have been learnt today. Nonetheless, Congolese authorities and international partners have proved powerless to harmonize institutional state-building initiatives (dominated largely by governance and security) with the physical rehabilitation of the country's woefully dilapidated infrastructure. The donor patchwork approach, the Herculean labour of physically reuniting the immense territory and political wrangling (largely bedevilled by the decentralization debate) account for this state reconstruction predicament. It is absurd to imagine that institutional reform and improved well-being can take place in a physically fragmented geography. Statehood is contingent upon people who adhere to the concept of belonging. Statehood is equally dependent upon a coherent unifying transportation network that provides mobility to traders, civil servants, political authorities, security forces and ordinary people. Without rehabilitation of the road-rail-river network, institutional reform efforts will remain sterile (Pourtier 2009, 1997).

Did the gradual degradation of infrastructure contribute to state collapse? Or, inversely, did state collapse lead to the neglect of infrastructure maintenance and the degradation witnessed all over the country? While these may be moot questions, the categorical imperative today is to consider territorial integration and state-building as inseparable. Not everyone accepts this argument. Congo, with its 2.3 million square kilometres, 4,700-kilometre-long river and 350 ethnic groups forming a population mosaic of approximately 67 million people is a 'charade' and should be abolished as a unitary state, according to Herbst and Mills (2009a, 2009b). As 'there is no Congo' in their view, they suggest that foreign governments should deal directly with those agents and institutions that are 'actually running' the country (meaning bilateral and international aid agencies, NGOs and churches) instead of focusing on rebuilding the Congolese state. They dispute the idea that 'one sovereign power is present in this vast country', arguing that any international efforts 'predicated on the Congo myth' are 'doomed to fail'. The tendency to advocate this form of Balkanization is based on a dubious cliché: Congo is too vast and too diverse to manage, an argument made for other large African states (Clapham et al. 2006). The tendency belittles a basic African fundamental. Although borders were indeed drawn artificially by Europeans in Berlin in 1885, people living within them – and Congolese are no exceptions – accept them. The map of Congo is undeniably branded in people's minds (Pourtier 2009).

Popular acceptance of a shared territory and internal recognition do not diminish the gigantic challenges confronted by reform planners. A first challenge is the extreme fragmentation of the country induced by ecological constraints. The vast central basin covered by dense humid forest and swampland is an age-old handicap to development. Movement of goods and people is limited because of the difficulties in travelling through what is an extremely inhospitable topography. The sparsely populated equatorial enclave of approximately one million square kilometres, inhabited by slash-and-burn farmers and indigenous peoples, deprives the country of a geographic and political centrality. Economic flows are centrifugal as opposed to centripetal, meaning that the periphery dominates the centre. This hinders economic development and makes state control of the territory practically impossible.

The soft forest underbelly separates the country more than it unites it and explains the emergence of an extraverted dynamism. The eastern provinces are more connected to Rwanda, Burundi, Tanzania and Uganda than they are to Kinshasa. It is economically more viable to export Katanga's minerals through Angola, Zambia and South Africa than through the distant Matadi port. Bas-Congo and Kinshasa owe their relative wealth to the narrow but precious 40-kilometre outlet to the Atlantic coast and the global markets that lie beyond. Traces of these spatial dynamics date as far back as the pre-colonial period, notably with respect to the powerful savannah kingdoms. Population density is high in these three peripheral zones because of ecology and the way that trade patterns have developed over time. Population density in the Kivus can reach up to one thousand inhabitants per square kilometre, which is a sharp contrast to the less than ten in the central basin. In geographical terms, this band of fragmented human settlements surrounding an underdeveloped basin resembles an immense archipelago (Bruneau and Simon 1991: 4). The country's urban settlements, which have the potential to revive commerce and mobility, are likewise disjointed. Overland travel between Kisangani and Mbuji-Mayi or Mbandaka and Lubumbashi, for example, is extremely difficult and time consuming.

The image of the Congo state is largely associated with Kinshasa, even though the Congolese capital lies on the fringe of the country. Kinshasa is a distant and abstract entity for many Congolese. A place of fascination and pleasure-seeking opportunities for some, it is a maelstrom of exploitation and corruption for others. As elsewhere in Africa, the degree of political and security control decreases in relation to the distance from the capital city (Herbst 2000; Bierschenk and Olivier de Sardan 1997). Rebellion in the Dongo region of Equateur province in 2010 proves this point. A conflict between local ethnic groups (the Enyele and Munzaya) began with a dispute over fishing rights but escalated because the Enyele were angry about the appointment of non-local representatives to the local administration. Insurgents confronted the police and very quickly overcame them. Without the support of MONUC blue helmets, the national army would have been ineffective.

Mobutu once toyed with the idea of transferring the seat of power from Kinshasa to Gbadolite, his now decrepit mini-Versailles in the jungle, but was unsuccessful. The political will of the dictator was unable to match the uncontrollable dynamics of the mega-city's expansion. In the early 1960s, independence leaders contemplated relocating the capital to the more central city of Luluabourg (today's Kananga). The idea was to bring the periphery closer to the centre of political and administrative power. A step in this direction had already been implemented in 1923 when Leopoldville replaced the even more peripheral Boma as colonial capital.

Another overwhelming challenge pertains to rehabilitating the transportation system. Without transportation there can be no mobility or development. Without transportation there can be no state. At independence, Congo had 145,000 kilometres of roads, 5,000 kilometres of rail and 15,000 kilometres of navigable rivers. These figures are still comparable but the quality has deteriorated. The number of airports and airstrips has more than doubled but the Congolese Civil Aviation Authority (RVA) is unable to respect security conditions established by the International Civil Aviation Organization. Congo's airspace is a black hole, holding the world record for the most aircraft crashes per year. This explains why MONUC set up its own air transport network and why it has become the principal provider of air transport in the country. The overall transportation network took years to set up and significant capital investment (which paid for itself through mineral exports). The colonial system of *cantonnage*, whereby each village was responsible for maintaining its own roads, was relatively efficient in keeping the roads open, but it was at the price of forced labour and the colonial whip. Europeans during the late colonial period could travel from Stanleyville (Kisangani) to Leopoldville (Kinshasa) in a Volkswagen Beetle in three days. This is absolutely inconceivable today and will remain so for many years to come.

Dugout canoes and bicycles are the principal means of transportation in much of rural Congo in the twenty-first century. In Goma, the emergence of handmade wooden scooters known as *cukudus* could be considered an inventive popular response to transportation needs. The *cukudu* could also be considered the emblem of pathetic regression. Traffic between major centres such as Tshikapa and Kananga (in Western Kasai province), each of which has a population of more than one million people, and which cross economically important areas, is only possible by bicycles, motorbikes and foot-porters. One positive development, however, is the increasing availability of relatively inexpensive motorbikes made in India (onomatopoeically called *tutu tuku* or *piki piki*).

Nationalization of the rail, river, sea and air transport companies following independence was the beginning of the end. Gradual decline continued in the mid-1970s as economic and political crisis deepened. As Belgian experts retired or returned to Belgium, competency was lost. Capacity-building in the Zaire of the time was not a priority in the transport sector. The nationalized transportation services (Onatra, SNCC, Office des routes, Régie des voies navigables and Régie des voies aériennes) became evermore corrupt and inefficient. As in other sectors, poorly paid employees lost motivation and used public services for private enrichment. Rolling stock became old, was poorly maintained and not replaced. By the end of the Mobutu dictatorship, Zaire had only 2,400 kilometres of tarmac road. This translates to 1 kilometre of modern road per 1,000 square kilometres of land surface, the lowest ratio in all of Africa (Pourtier 2009: 36). Owing mainly to European Union funding, Congo now has 3,000 kilometres of tarmac road (International Bank for Reconstruction and Development/World Bank 2010: 9). Road building and maintenance in the Congo are also confronted by a serious ecological difficulty. Sandy soil and heavy rains are not conducive to tarmac unless it is meticulously maintained. Broken bridges and ferries were not replaced, making mobility an ordeal in a land criss-crossed by thousands of small rivers and streams.

Only eight out of twelve docks at the Matadi port were operational in 2006 (République démocratique du Congo 2006: 35). Instead of capitalizing on its position of sea-rail-road hub, the Matadi port is more often associated with administrative hassles, bottlenecks and logistical weaknesses. Even the geographic conditions of Matadi (which is upstream from the mouth of the Congo river) are handicaps to the port's development. Because of the strong currents, large cargo ships have difficulty navigating it, which accounts for future plans to invest in the deep-water port of Banana, closer to the coast. By the time the two regional wars ended and the transitional government was put in place in 2002, the transportation network had been destroyed. Traffic congestion in Kinshasa has become a nightmare: Kinois say 'we know when we leave home but have no idea when we will get to where we want to go'. Congo is becoming more and more immense as it takes longer and longer to get from one point to another.

An important strategic document elaborated by Congolese authorities with the support of World Bank experts outlined objectives for growth and poverty reduction. It emphasized five priorities: good governance and peace, macroeconomic stability, improved access to social services, dealing with HIV/AIDS and supporting community development. It is noteworthy that rehabilitation of the transportation network was not indicated as a priority. The document severely criticized the sector's inefficient management, outdated regulatory framework and absence of coherent vision (ibid.: 35). It is rather uncommon to find such a blunt evaluation in an official Congolese government document. The government's development programme for the period 2007–11 did, however, identify transportation as a priority, and infrastructure rehabilitation was targeted in President Kabila's *cinq chantiers* development package launched in 2008.

Congo's international partners have been involved in the transportation challenge for years. The European Commission launched an infrastructure rehabilitation programme (*Programme d'appui à la réhabilitation*) in the mid-1990s which had the ambition of rehabilitating nearly seven thousand kilometres of roads, but war interrupted the programme. Today, along with the World Bank and the European Commission, which are the main protagonists in transport rehabilitation, the African Development Bank and Belgian, British, German and Kuwaiti partners provide support. China is a relatively new partner which has earmarked important resources for road and infrastructure construction and maintenance ($3 billion) in exchange for minerals. In 2008 the government established a national road maintenance funding mechanism (*Fonds national d'entretien routier*). PRO-ROUTES, a major road upgrade project in the DRC, was launched in August 2009. Its ambitiously declared aim is to promote economic growth by making movement easier across the entire country. Funded mainly by the World Bank and the United Kingdom, it seeks to reinforce the operational capacity of Congolese structures in charge of the road network and to enable the reopening of principal road links and their continued maintenance. Congolese counterparts in these initiatives are the Ministry of Infrastructure Public Works and Reconstruction and the Ministry of Transportation. As rural feeder roads are an area of particular concentration, the Ministry of Agriculture is also involved. Strategies evolve rather quickly in this sector because of funding concerns and donor agendas but a number of priorities have been identified.

With respect to roads, a first phase aims at uniting all of the provincial capitals among themselves and with Kinshasa. A second phase will be creating feeder roads from rural hinterlands and connecting them to those roads targeted during the first phase. The cost of road work in DRC is particularly expensive owing to logistical and ecological considerations. Belgian Technical Cooperation paid $3,100 per kilometre for construction and maintenance of dirt track in forest areas between 2006 and 2009. The price was $2,700 in savannah areas. Tarmac is considerably more expensive and not always the best value for money. The costs are augmented owing to the paucity of competitive private construction companies. Forrest, Safricas and BIA are among the few companies eligible to tender for publicly funded infrastructure projects. These few big public works players are increasingly subcontracting to smaller local companies. To diminish the impact of this absorption-capacity handicap, donors tend to enter into partnerships with local NGOs, which hire large numbers of unskilled workers who are paid very low wages (approximately $1 per day) or even paid in food, to implement road rehabilitation and maintenance. This labour-intensive approach (known by the French acronym HIMO, *haute intensité de main-d'oeuvre*) promotes the use of basic tools such as machetes, shovels and picks, as opposed to mechanized equipment.

The Matadi–Lubumbashi highway has received the greater part of donor funding. The 3,000-kilometre route serves the double purpose of linking the Atlantic port to the mineral production area of the country while connecting a series of important cities: Banana, Moanda, Boma, Matadi, Mbanza-Ngungu, Madimba, Kinshasa, Kenge, Kikwit, Tshikapa, Bulungu, Kananga, Mbuji-Mayi, Mwene-Ditu, Kamina, Bukama, Lubudi, Likasi, Lubumbashi and Sakania. A second objective relates to national sovereignty. In terms of cost and logistics it could be more efficient to export Katanga's mineral wealth through South Africa, Angola or Tanzania, but relying on the national transport network makes more sense from a national development perspective. The paving of the 800-kilometre stretch between Beni and Kisangani is a recent accomplishment that has contributed to opening up Kisangani to East Africa. Throughout much of the country some road work has been ongoing thanks to international funding, but the overall result is far from contributing to a strategy of national integration. In some cases, road work is based primarily on facilitating mineral exports while in other instances it is based on local political constituency building. While road-building and rehabilitation are absolute necessities, donors are increasingly attentive to the direct and indirect impacts this work could have on people and the environment. The British government has consequently funded the elaboration of impact assessment methods to mitigate the negative impacts that roads could have (DfID and Environment and Development Group 2008). The British Department for International Development (DfID) is also working closely with the Congolese government to monitor the impacts that Chinese infrastructure projects could have. Three per cent of each project in the Congo–China infrastructure deal is supposed to be spent on environmental mitigation (Brautigan 2009: 303).

Congo's railway system is in a dire state of disrepair. The 5,000-kilometre network is comprised of three sub-networks: (i) the Kinshasa–Matadi line (operated by Onatra – Office national des transports), (ii) a 3,641-kilometre sub-network linking Katanga with Kanaga and Ilebo in the Kasai provinces and Zambia and Angola (operated by SNCC – Société nationale des chemins de fer du Congo) and (iii) the remnants of the CFU (Chemin de fer des Ueles) in the north-east. Relatively little funding has been made available to improve the Congolese railways, although there has been some technical and administrative support for the rail network operators along with capacity-building efforts. The Belgian government sponsored the rehabilitation of an important rail bridge over the Nyemba river in Katanga, facilitating traffic between the port of Kalemie and Kabolo. The full benefits of this investment have not been felt because of siltation at the Kalemie port. Siltation makes it difficult for large vessels coming across Lake Tanganyika from East Africa to dock. Plans to dredge the port have not moved forward. Likewise, talks about revamping the Kinshasa urban train system have been ongoing for years but work has not started.

The majestic Congo river is often considered the lifeline of the country, serving as a link between road and rail networks. River and lake transport take place mainly between Kinshasa and Kisangani, Kinshasa and Ilebo and on Lakes Tanganyika and Kivu. While the Congo river and its numerous tributaries are used extensively by local people for transportation, three major obstacles hamper its contribution to economic development (Loore 2007). The first is geographic. It does not go through the country's most populated areas or the zones where human and economic activity are most dynamic, such as the Kivus, the Kasais or Katanga. Secondly, the river is underexploited by the big potential users such as ONATRA, Gécamines and the National River Agency (RVF).

The fleet of ships and barges is old and mostly inoperative, and the ports are in a serious state of disrepair and decay. Instead of using the Congo river to export its minerals through Matadi, for example, Gécamines exports through Dar es Salaam in Tanzania. The RVF is unable to dredge, buoy and mark the river ways because its equipment is obsolete. This makes river transport dangerous, which also accounts for the numerous accidents that are frequently reported. Thirdly, river traffic, like so many other aspects of daily life in Congo, is subject to administrative hassles by the numerous state agencies that are involved in monitoring the circulations of goods and people, the *tracasseries* that Rackley (2006) appropriately documented.

Corruption, inefficiency and mismanagement are constant obstacles to the successful implementation of transport and infrastructure rehabilitation. Acting on behalf of the World Bank and the African Development Bank, the Coordination Bureau (BCECO) is the Congolese executing agency that coordinates international financial aid allocated for a wide range of development projects. But the BCECO has the notorious reputation of perpetuating inefficient and corrupt practices. A consultant working for the World Bank reported that it tolerated irregular procedures by BCECO. Two years after signing contracts for the rehabilitation of two highways only 10 per cent of the work was completed, even though the planning was for a total of eighteen months. The government, moreover, succeeded in squashing the decision to hire a World Bank expert as BCECO assistant director (de Villers 2009: 363). These are good examples of both extraversion and masquerade.

Funding pledges by international partners for infrastructure development are not enough, which is another serious challenge. The amounts required would absorb almost all the national budget.

To rebuild the country and catch up with the rest of the developing world, the DRC needs to spend $5.3 billion a year over the next decade, or 75 per cent of the 2006 GDP. Of this total, as much as $1.1 billion a year needs to be devoted to maintenance alone. The DRC's recent infrastructure spending of $700 million a year – even though it represents 10 per cent of GDP – falls far below the level needed to make an impact over the next decade. Significant inefficiencies are wasting resources worth at least $430 million each year, but even if these problems were corrected, an infrastructure funding gap of the order of $4 billion a year would remain (International Bank for Reconstruction and Development/World Bank 2010: 1).

The challenge of reuniting the Congolese territory through a viable transportation network is enormous. Congolese authorities and international partners have come to recognize it as an absolute priority because all of the other reform initiatives depend on it. There can be no security without transportation, no economic growth, no public administration and no sentiment of national unity. Territorial integration exemplifies the necessity to consider state-building in a holistic way. Efforts at territorial reunification require significant funding and viable mechanisms to ensure proper maintenance. While this is necessary, it is not enough. The real issue is one of governance. International partners can help but they cannot replace the Congolese state; nor can they afford to underestimate the power of the political and administrative culture that governs the multiple agencies that should be the drivers of piecing the patchwork back together.

Security sector reform

Although the Global and Inclusive Peace Agreement was signed in 2002, security has yet to return to the Congo. On the contrary, politically orchestrated insecurity prevails. It is fuelled by the pillaging of natural resources, a reality well documented by the United Nations' group of experts on the Democratic Republic of the Congo (United Nations Panel of Inquiry 2009). When this report was released, UN secretary-general Ban Ki-moon could not avoid referring to the situation as 'a humanitarian crisis of catastrophic dimensions'.

Historically entrenched tit-for-tat violence in the Great Lakes region has had a devastating effect on the Congolese population, mainly but not exclusively in the eastern provinces. The two Congo wars (1996/97 and 1998–2003) are believed to have resulted in an estimated 5.4 million 'excess deaths', according to the International Rescue Committee (2008),[1] although the figures are contested by certain demographic experts (Lambert and Lohlé-Tart 2008). The arrival of more than one million Hutu refugees from Rwanda in 1994 exacerbated the context of violence and insecurity. One of the world's worst humanitarian disasters since the Second World War took place in Congo during this period. The improvement of human security and the establishment of state authority throughout the country thus remain major national and regional priorities. The international community has invested significantly in this process, particularly through security sector reform.

Internationally supported initiatives to facilitate the peace process and promote regional stability included the Comité international d'accompagnement de la transition (CIAT),[2] the World Bank 'Multi-Country Demobilization and Reintegration Programme' (MDRP) and the International Conference for the African Great Lakes Region (ICGLR). This international commitment helped establish some political stability and economic recovery and ensured the functioning of transitional institutions. It facilitated the preparation of the 2006 elections and encouraged the redefinition of regional relations based on integration and cooperation. Belgium, France, South Africa, the European Union, Angola and MONUC were the main international actors in security sector reform. France and Angola collaborated in training the Police d'intervention rapide, a special police unit. The UK, the USA and the Netherlands were also involved to a lesser degree.

Efforts to reform the security sector took place in two distinct phases.[3] The first phase overlapped with the period of political transition from 2001 to 2006. The Global and All-Inclusive Agreement signed in December 2002 included an entire chapter on security sector reform. This chapter proposed to form an integrated national army, including the main rebel movements, and set up a high-level body (the Conseil supérieur de la défense), which was to have a mandate to declare war, advise on national defence priorities, security sector reform and disarmament, demobilization and reintegration (DDR). However, no action was taken on these proposals for three years, owing largely to the absence of political will. President Kabila and his vice-presidents were unwilling to compromise control over their combatants and there was a lack of coordination between national and international partners. It was also during this period that the UN, the World Bank and the European Commission in partnership with Kinshasa agreed upon a 'governance compact' in which security sector reform was identified as a priority. As with other such agreements, results never materialized.

In June 2003 an agreement was reached by Kabila, Vice-President Ruberwa and Vice-President Bemba about the distribution of senior army and security positions in the high command of the integrated army. The following month, an oversight body was constituted to monitor integration of the police and army. In early 2004 a system was devised to dismantle parallel command structures controlled by former belligerents in an attempt to merge them into a single national army, while attempting to create an *esprit de corps*. A specific action was the Belgian-funded training exercise of the first integrated brigade which took place in Kisangani in February 2004.

The year 2005 was an important one for security sector reform in Congo. It received a boost from new donors (notably the United Kingdom), which came to realize that the lack of security was hampering all other institutional reform efforts. International partners thus sought to give the integration plan new impetus (while Congolese political leaders only gave lip-service to the idea). The plan aimed at regrouping and disarming former combatants, informing them about DDR through awareness campaigns and reintegrating them into a unified army in a *brassage* centre, or reintegrating them into society (through work and training programmes), depending on their choice. *Brassage* refers to the process of integrating the different Congolese armed groups into a national army. Its main objective was to dismantle the chains of command of the previously warring groups. This was a daunting challenge because political and military factions were unwilling to relinquish control over their militias. The vice-presidents of the Mouvement pour la libération du Congo (MLC) and the Rassemblement congolais pour la démocratie-Goma (RCD-G), Jean-Pierre Bemba and Azarias Ruberwa, were protected by their own faithfuls. These militiamen and Kabila's Republican Guard, whose members were recruited largely in Katanga and the Kivus, were not subject to *brassage* at this stage.

The European Union carried out two advisory missions in mid-2005: the European Union police mission (EUPOL) (Vircoulon 2009a) and the European Union mission to provide advice and assistance to security sector reform (EUSEC) (Clément 2009a). During the transition EUPOL oversaw the EU-trained integrated police unit. This was a serious priority because Jean-Pierre Bemba, Azarias Ruberwa and Joseph Kabila all had rival militias present in the city. The volatile security situation had the potential to upset the electoral process. Following elections, EUPOL offered support for the structural reform of the Congolese national police force (Police nationale congolaise). If EUPOL's formal mandate was the improved decision-making and supervision of police units, in fact, '... the mission served politics in both Kinshasa and Brussels. Kinshasa could claim the mission as part of its democratic credentials while the EU promoted it as evidence of the reality of the European Defence and Security Policy, within which it was framed' (Hills 2009: 176). EUSEC was a small, civilian advisory mission on army reform in the DRC whose tasks included designing workable strategies to pay soldiers. Police and military racketeering and violence perpetrated against civilians are often explained by the fact that security forces are poorly paid, or not paid at all. They live off the population, which is a legacy of the Mobutu dictatorship. His military was unprofessional, undisciplined, fragmented, poorly organized, corrupt and predatory. This situation is largely the same years after reform efforts commenced.

The second phase of efforts to reform the security sector started in the run-up to the 2006 elections. There was some success in putting troops under a unified command structure and

President Kabila was able to marginalize former vice-presidents Azarias Ruberwa and Jean-Pierre Bemba. According to Clément (2009b: 94), this was a period when '[p]olitical opposition [...] was muted in Kinshasa'. However, the Congolese army was struggling to bring peace to North Kivu. Two highly effective and violent rebel groups continued to wreak havoc there. One was Laurent Nkunda's Rwanda-backed Congrès national pour la défense du peuple (CNDP), which also had the support of extremist remnants of the Rassemblement congolais pour la démocratie, including powerful Congolese officers of Tutsi origin like Nkunda himself. The other was the resilient Forces démocratiques de libération du Rwanda (FDLR). Kinshasa was eventually to strike a deal with CNDP leaders, who accepted the idea of a new version of *brassage*, called *mixage*. Unlike the *brassage* strategy, which had proven largely unsuccessful, *mixage* was mainly a Kivu-based strategy aimed at integrating senior officers in brigades but not attempting to integrate foot soldiers.

Security sector reform struggled to keep up with a seriously challenged peace process hampered by new security threats in the east. After having failed to make progress through military actions, Kinshasa adopted a political approach based on regional cooperation. An important meeting took place in Nairobi in November 2007 which resulted in a botched trade-off agreement between Congo and Rwanda. The Congolese army would take a firmer stance against the FDLR and Rwanda would put pressure on the CNDP to cease hostilities. The January 2008 meeting in Goma, attended by the different armed groups, Congolese parliamentarians, civil society representatives and international observers, reiterated and confirmed support for these deals. Fighting continued, however, because the CNDP was not committed to finding a solution and the process was underfunded by international partners. Another year of violence went by before a solution was found. Sweden, the Netherlands, the United States and the United Kingdom put financial pressure on the Kigali government. As a result, a secret deal was made between Presidents Kagame and Kabila in January 2009 allowing Rwandese armed troops to enter and operate in the DRC.

This joint Congolese–Rwandese offensive resulted in months of operations against the FDLR and the capture of Laurent Nkunda. Two operations were subsequently organized in an attempt to dismantle the FDLR, *Kimia II* and *Umoja Wetu*. Another operation, *Amani Leo*, began at the start of 2010 and aimed at protecting civilian populations. It was also aimed at holding territory liberated from armed groups like the FDLR and helping to restore state authority. Despite these efforts, a UN report concludes that operations against the FDLR failed to dismantle the organization's political and military structures and that it continues to benefit from support from top commanders of the Congolese national army (FARDC), some of whom are former supporters of Laurent Nkunda (United Nations Panel of Inquiry 2009). There is evidence that most of the FARDC units now in the Kivus are Rwandaphone, which is an additional source of friction with the local population. Nkunda's arrest was part of a larger deal made between Kigali and Kinshasa. One trade-off was integrating former CNDP chief of staff Bosco Ntaganda into the Congolese national army with the rank of general. Ntaganda, also known as 'the terminator', is wanted by the International Criminal Court for the war crimes of enlisting and conscripting children under the age of fifteen and using them to participate actively in hostilities.[4]

In addition to these specific actions, design of security sector reform has been ongoing. A strategic master plan for the armed services (*Schéma directeur de la réforme des forces armées*) was prepared in late 2007. Its four objectives were: (i) the setting up of a rapid reaction force of two or three battalions to prepare for the gradual withdrawal of MONUC forces; (ii) to instil 'an ideal of excellence' through improved training and military justice mechanisms; (iii) to improve relations between military forces and the civilian population; and (iv) to put the army to work in the development sector (public works and agriculture, for example) (Hoebeke et al. 2009). Infighting between senior Congolese authorities (due in part to ministerial reshuffling in late 2008) and lack of donor enthusiasm condemned this plan at the outset. A revised plan of army reform was developed by military attachés, MONUC and the EU, and was approved by President Kabila in May 2009. Also, a body was set up to coordinate national and international security actions: the Comité de suivi de la réforme de l'armée.

Two overwhelming urgencies have not been resolved. One, armed forces continue to perpetrate violence, rape and other forms of abusive behaviour towards civilians. They are corrupt and use guns to illegally exploit minerals. Margot Wallstrom, the UN's special representative on sexual violence in conflict, called the Congo 'the rape capital of the world': more than eight thousand women were raped in 2009.[5] Two, security sector reform is trapped in a catch-22 conundrum: protracted violence prevents the implementation of state authority, while the weakness and ineffectiveness of state institutions exacerbate the violence perpetrated by armed groups. Another obstacle has been analysed with finesse by Hoebeke et al. (ibid.: 119). They confirm that Congolese local and national actors prefer organizing insecurity rather than improving security: it facilitates the unregulated exploitation of natural resources and maintains disorder in territories where they can levy illegal taxes.

These examples prove that the whole security sector reform process was flawed at the outset. Far from being a mere technical or operational challenge, it has been a highly politicized one (Clément 2009b: 90). Vetting, a non-legal process of screening security forces for past crimes and abuses, and control strategies are practically non-existent. These are serious oversights given the extreme secrecy and corruption that are inherent in the Congo's security establishment. Military justice and women's rights have been largely neglected. The large number of Congolese, bilateral and multilateral actors in this arena do not share common vision or objectives. A major flaw was the lack of commitment on the part of Congolese authorities to accept the process. According to Melmot (2008), it has been an imported policy that was never appropriated by local stakeholders. For Vircoulon (2009b: 226), 'police reform is more an initiative of the donors than the DRC government'.

Another flaw pertains to the disparity between bilateral and multilateral approaches. Congolese authorities (and some of Congo's long-standing partners such as Belgium) preferred a bilateral approach. In its Mobutu-style playing of one international partner off against another, this classic strategy of extraversion enabled them to maintain a certain degree of independence and manipulate international partners. They did so in this instance by putting forward the sacrosanct argument of national sovereignty. They argued that the multilateral approach was less sensitive to the need to respect national sovereignty, that it was more cumbersome to coordinate and that it lacked coherence. According to one well-informed source, advocating bilateral military cooperation was a strategy 'to postpone reforms' (International Crisis Group 2007: 22).

None of these plans, agreements and operations has succeeded in reforming the Congolese security sector. Each has failed to protect ordinary people. The president himself has indirectly made clear that he does not trust the national army. Like Mobutu, who depended on the feared Special Presidential Division, Kabila relies on his Angolan-trained Republican Guard for his personal security. He controls this special unit of some ten thousand troops himself, without bothering with the national army's chain of command. These are yet other examples that support the argument that reform initiatives are masquerade. Confirming this conclusion, the question has been raised of whether or not the whole conflict resolution process has been 'a realistic goal or just snake oil sold by smooth operators' (Prunier 2009: 329).

United Nations peacekeeping

Discussion of security sector reform goes hand in hand with the United Nations Organization Mission in the Democratic Republic of Congo (MONUC). Operational since November 1999, MONUC is often perceived as being as much a part of a security problem in the Great Lakes region as an actor in problem-solving. Well-informed sources – including the UN itself – have accused the mission of sexual abuse of children, gold and diamond smuggling, arms trading and running away from rebels – with whom they also share intelligence. It is criticized for being ineffective, politically biased and expensive. The 2010 budget was over $1.3 billion, which represents approximately one sixth of the UN's peacekeeping budget. 'Critics contend that nowhere else in the world has the United Nations invested so much and accomplished so little' (Gettleman 2010).

Protecting civilian lives is the most important task of MONUC. In this respect it has utterly failed. Its institutional and operational links with the national army raise serious doubts about the UN mission because the national army is increasingly the major perpetrator of human rights abuses, ahead even of rebel groups. In the complex Congolese environment, the UN mission is 'mission impossible'. Created to monitor the implementation of the Lusaka Peace Accord, its current mandate includes monitoring ceasefires between foreign and Congolese forces, disarming and repatriating foreign armed combatants, assisting the transition to democratic rule and helping the government dismantle remaining armed groups in the Kivus and Ituri. This mandate is tantamount to authorizing the UN to play a strategic role in the reconstruction and reform process. It also supports the argument that the Congo is in a position of neo-trusteeship because the mandate shifts sovereignty responsibilities away from the government to an international body.

Another problem with the MONUC mandate pertains to implementation and interpretation. Peacekeepers are often confused about what they should do and how they should work. Security Council decisions are not always translated into precise operational guidelines for implementation. The Congo situation confirms the argument of a researcher who has studied a number of UN missions: '[I]n the absence of clear directives and uniform methodology and criteria for action, there are often as many interpretations of a mandate as there are members of a mission' (Pouligny 2006: 119).

MONUC's presence in Congo has traces of déjà vu. The UN was previously engaged in a peacekeeping mission during the

Congolese post-independence crisis between 1960 and 1964. At that time, this was also the UN's largest deployment of troops. The UN carried out some of its most controversial actions, notably political bias against democratically elected prime minister Lumumba and favouritism towards the European mining interests that supported the Katanga secession. When the Security Council approved the mission, its mandate was to restore law and order and maintain it; stop other nations from getting involved in the crisis; assist in building the nation's economy; and restore political stability (Lefever 1967). Almost immediately, things went wrong for the United Nations force – and for the Congolese people. Although the country did not descend into outright civil war, Lumumba was assassinated, the country became a major stake in East–West rivalry at the height of the Cold War, and the foundation for one of Africa's most notorious dictatorships was laid.

From an original force of 5,537 troops and 500 military observers, the United Nations Security Council steadily increased MONUC's presence until 2010. The world's largest UN mission had 20,573 uniformed personnel in 2010, plus 1,001 international civilian personnel, 2,690 local civilian staff and 629 United Nations Volunteers (MONUC 2009). Nevertheless, a troop increase (in other words, a military strategy) cannot solve the intractable problems of endemic violence and corruption. Working towards a political process of engagement would be a more logical alternative (Zeebroek 2009). UN agencies, however, are not well equipped financially and conceptually to integrate this longer-term approach. An analysis presented by Autesserre (2010: 95) supports this view: 'the main reason that the peace-building strategy in Congo has failed is that the international community has paid too little attention to the root causes of violence there: local disputes over land and power'. Cynics could argue that troop increases have been in reverse proportion to the achievement of results. Indeed, challenges have outpaced the objectives of 'peace-building' and 'peacekeeping'. The nuanced difference between these two terms is that the former has a governance connotation while the latter pertains more directly to security issues. MONUC also claims to be involved in a 'peace enforcement' phase through its efforts at helping the government dismantle the FDLR (the last significant rebel challenge to its authority), protect vulnerable communities from rebel violence and establish state authority and the rule of law.

Translating rhetoric into action has not been easy for MONUC but the mission can claim some achievements. It has participated in peace-building and the reluctant transition towards democratic rule by overseeing the implementation of the Lusaka Agreement and facilitating the Sun City national dialogue. It provided crucial logistical support for the 2006 elections, and continues to help coordinate humanitarian aid and the monitoring of human rights abuses. From a security perspective MONUC has monitored ceasefires between foreign and Congolese forces, brokered local truces between rival groups in the Kivus and disarmed and repatriated thousands of foreign armed combatants. It has also successfully helped the government dismantle armed groups in the Kivus and Ituri.

The aviation sector has played a major role in reuniting this huge and fragmented territory through the transportation of goods and people. As DRC has the world's worst record for aircraft crashes, this contribution is not trivial. In addition to transporting its own military and civilian staff, MONUC flights carry government officials, international experts and civil society representatives. It has even relocated endangered mountain gorillas to a North Kivu nature park.[6] Radio Okapi is another MONUC achievement. The radio was originally set up in 2000 (with the Swiss Hirondelle Foundation) to inform the Congolese people about the transition process. It remains one of the best sources of information today.

Although perceptions of MONUC vary considerably from east to west, there are some clearly identifiable patterns. MONUC protects, yes, but it also disturbs because of its arrogance and inefficiency. It contributes to a fragile stability but at the cost of intruding into the lives of people while trespassing into the domains of national sovereignty. While the mission has participated in the

69

process of democratic transition, it has not improved standards of living or well-being (Zeebroek 2009: 151). People have also come to realize that MONUC blue helmets do not want to die for the Congo. These perceptions reveal that people have had unrealistic expectations. As they do not trust their own leaders to solve their problems, hope that the UN mission could do so was high. That hope has obviously not been satisfied.

Official discourse in the early phases of the mission was designed to justify its presence. It was necessary because legacies of war persisted. These included the illegal exploitation of natural resources, weak government capacity (which has limited impact outside Kinshasa), ethnic differences and land disputes, perpetration with impunity of human rights violations against the most vulnerable segments of society, and the presence of heavily armed rebels who continue to challenge state authority. Until 2009, the Congolese government subscribed – or at least acquiesced – to this view. Today, however, the manipulation of discourse has become much more complex.

The Congolese government is trying to reassure the population that it has the security situation under control. This is an important prerequisite for electoral success in the 2011 elections and explains the wide divergence between NGO reports on casualties during the Easter 2010 uprising in Equateur province and government statements that tried to downplay them. For the fifty-year independence ceremonies, the government wanted to announce that MONUC was no longer needed, which could have had a positive populist impact. Nevertheless, beyond what has become a frequently vitriolic 'MONUC go home' discourse, there is no certainty that the government really wants the mission to withdraw. It does not have the security situation under control and MONUC forces could help the government save face in the future, as they did during the Equateur uprising.

A compromise on withdrawal is being designed: the UN has responded to Congolese requests by gradually starting troop withdrawal. Two thousand troops withdrew in July 2010 and the operation was rebaptized MONUSCO (Mission des nations unies pour la stabilisation du Congo). A United Nations stabilization mission thus replaced the peacekeeping one. The Security Council made it clear to the Congolese government that full withdrawal would be contingent on progress in the restoration of state authority and reduction in violence. More specifically, this pragmatic process will be based on the Congolese capacity to protect civilians and fight against sexual violence, effective training of police officers, and defeating rebel groups (mainly the Forces démocratiques de libération du Rwanda and the Lord's Resistance Army). Designing a meaningful exit strategy is not going to be easy because MONUSCO is confronted by a difficult paradox. If it stays, it will continue to artificially replace the state in the crucial security sector; if it leaves, a security vacuum could result with the likelihood of increased armed conflict. This raises another difficult question: is Congo a post-conflict country or a pre-conflict one?

Decentralization

The aborted decentralization process is another convincing illustration of the Congo masquerade. It reveals how an important constitutional commitment was made without taking into account overwhelming administrative, political and macroeconomic challenges. The commitment was also made without thinking through the mechanisms and technicalities of implementation. A comparative, historical study of decentralization shows that low-income countries emerging from conflict rarely have the human and material resources to make decentralization happen (Marysse 2005: 206). It should have been obvious at the outset, given the extent of state collapse, that Congo would not have the means or the political will to decentralize.

In addition to the absence of political will, challenges were exacerbated by the significant regional diversities in terms of natural wealth and revenue generation. Congo's international partners involved in institutional reform share responsibility in the failure of decentralization because they have not been sufficiently engaged in the process. Another major but often underestimated problem relates to the 'Berlin Conference syndrome': proposed territorial demarcations do not correspond to linguistic and ethnic realities, which is a serious threat to political, social and economic viability. Disconnect between decentralization and the necessity to reorganize the role and structure of the civil service is yet another absurdity. Territorial decentralization cannot work without a decentralized civil service. Nonetheless, little attention has been given to this disconnect by the central government and international partners.

When the Congolese people ratified the 2006 constitution they were promised greater local-level autonomy within a three-year period. They are still waiting. This can be summarized as 'decide first, negotiate later'. The constitution maintained the subdivision of the country into the eleven provinces inherited by previous governments; it also added two important new elements. First, territorial decentralization was introduced, in theory to allocate greater financial autonomy and resource management to the provinces than in the past. After years of corrupt, centralized rule, voters welcomed the prospect of participating in the local-level decision-making process. Decentralization and democratization were perceived as being elements of the same process, even though it seems that most ordinary people and many elected politicians do not really understand what their rights and responsibilities would be in a new decentralized landscape. Secondly, within a three-year period, the eleven provinces were mandated to be redivided into twenty-six. The boundaries of these twenty-six provinces were to follow current administrative divisions, mainly redefining 'districts' as new provinces. The deadline for this transition from eleven to twenty-six provinces as stipulated in the constitution has passed and the process is at a standstill. This created political fury in December 2009, not least because it entailed discussions about amending the constitution.[7] The debate resurfaced in March 2010 when the president of the National Assembly and Kabila ally Evariste Boshab argued that revision of the constitution (including the length of the presidential mandate) is legal because the constitution 'must adapt to the reality of the Congolese population' (Dabo 2010).

From the Kinshasa perspective, decentralization is antithetical to its efforts to consolidate power. The government's objective is to capture and secure power, not redistribute it. A system has to be strong to share power; the Congolese government is too vulnerable to share. A concomitant problem is the absence of capacity to absorb new administrative and governance responsibilities at the provincial level. While provincial authorities wanted power, they would be unable to manage it. Administrative staff, infrastructure and material resources are not available in most provinces. According to one Congolese political scientist, 80 per cent of the provincial representatives are new to politics. As they lack political savvy, the wilier Kinshasa governing establishment is able to take advantage of their naivety. Kinshasa controls and manipulates the debate because it distributes salaries and perks to these new political actors (J. Omasombo, interviewed in Cros 2010b). Kabila is reproducing Mobutu-style tactics of selectively distributing funds to the provinces in exchange for political loyalty. The World Bank and the IMF have also proved reluctant to support decentralization. While they have a relatively firm grip on the macro-financial situation in Kinshasa, control in the provinces escapes them.

Decentralization is a complicated political process that requires the commitment and involvement of both central government and provincial authorities. It cannot take place in a democratic vacuum where political actors ignore – or disdain – the principles of accountability. The process requires the establishment of overlapping interests and the achievement of mutual trust between the central government and representatives from the decentralized entities. The concepts of solidarity and consensus will have to be reintroduced into the Congolese political lexicon if decentralization is to take form. Post-conflict DRC was just not ready to meet these conditions. This reality led to the resignation of the governors of South Kivu and Maniema in April 2010.[8]

Defining the territorial map of Congo has been a long, complicated and still-unresolved struggle dating back to the Leopoldian period. In 1888 the Congo Free State was comprised of eleven districts: four more were added in 1895. In 1910, the year after the Congo became a Belgian colony, the territory was divided into twelve districts. In 1913 these twelve districts were redefined and became four provinces. Two more provinces were configured in 1933, resulting in the six-province map that lasted until after decolonization. The territorial mosaic continued to shift under Mobutu. The 1964 Luluabourg constitution provided for twenty-one provinces (*provincettes*), but Mobutu backtracked in 1966 when Zaire reconfigured into eight provinces. This constant need to draw and redraw the administrative map is based on ethnic pressures, regional affiliations and the need to accommodate political alliances. The difficult quest for a viable territorial logic also testifies to the fact that, historically, the territory was not colonized in a unified, systematic way: the colonial territorial administration was ad hoc and arbitrary. This legacy continues to influence today's negotiations.

The debate between Congolese authorities who advocate a federal (decentralized) political system, in opposition to a strong centralized regime, has been ongoing since independence. In the early 1960s, the main supporters of federalism emerged from political parties from Bas-Congo, Bandundu, the southern areas of the then-unified Kasai and Katanga. Supporters of a strong centralized state (referred to as 'unitarists') came from Oriental province and the Kivus. This cleavage illustrates – then and now – that richer provinces tend to support federalism so they can have greater autonomy in retaining and controlling their own resources. The Katanga secession in 1960 was an extreme manifestation of this perspective. Poorer areas support a strong centralized state, contending that the central government should redistribute wealth on an egalitarian basis. Radical nationalists led by the 'unitarist' prime minister, Patrice Lumumba, considered that federalism was a neocolonial tactic to weaken the newly independent country. Their reasoning was based on France's Balkanization of French West Africa and French Equatorial Africa.

In addition to these political challenges, resolving the financial technicalities of decentralization has proved particularly difficult for the Congolese government. Attention has focused largely on one number: forty. According to Article 175 of the constitution, the central government receives 50 per cent of revenues and the provinces 40 per cent. The original – but politically contentious – feature of this 40 per cent pertains to the fact that the provinces are mandated to retain these revenues instead of authorizing Kinshasa to collect them under the condition that they will be retransferred (a fiscal and legal mechanism referred to as retrocession). The problem results from the tax collection system. National revenues in Congo are collected by the central government through specialized collection structures, mainly OFIDA (customs and excise tax), DGRAD (fees and commissions), DGI and DGE (income tax). In the current context, a mining or logging company pays its taxes to the central government and, in theory, the central government gives back to the provinces a percentage of revenues. According to the new logic, these companies will pay 40 per cent of their taxes directly to the provinces and the remainder to Kinshasa. However, before the new logic can be effective a new tax collection system has to be devised. But parliamentary commissions working on this important fiscal priority have not made progress. Another problem results from the distrust that exists between centre and periphery. In the years prior to the elections, the central government transferred approximately 20 per cent of national revenues to the provinces. In 2007, this amount was arbitrarily reduced to between 6 and 7 per cent (Verheijen 2008: 3). Another ambiguity pertains to revenues that cannot be attributed to a specific province: Congo's offshore oil production, for example. These issues were studies by a special commission (*Commission paritaire*) comprised of representatives from the central government, provincial governors and provincial assemblies, but again, nothing tangible has resulted from their deliberations.

While the prospect of being able to retain 40 per cent of revenues may be perceived as an advantage to some provincial leaders, there are also significant drawbacks. Responsibilities, results and deliverables accompany rights. But local self-governing powers do not have the capacity to absorb new social, security and administrative responsibilities. Establishing mechanisms to share revenues is already considerably complex; redefining who does what in terms of service provision is even more difficult. Forty per cent may seem like a large amount of money, but there are no guarantees that it will be enough to cover all the costs for the services that the new provinces are supposed to provide. Provincial responsibilities include almost all expenses relating to primary and secondary education, salaries of civil servants and healthcare. Large provinces with high population density and scant resources will simply not be able to cope.

Article 175 of the constitution also stipulates that 10 per cent of national revenues go to a *caisse de péréquation*. This is an equalizing mechanism to enable poorer provinces to benefit from the resources of the richer ones. It is important because 80 per cent of national wealth emanates from only two provinces: mineral-rich Katanga and Bas-Congo, where the Inga dam and the Matadi port are located.[9] Many of the poorer provinces (Haut-Uele, Bas-Uele and Nord-Ubangi, for example) are not economically viable because they do not have high-value or easily extractable natural resources, financial capacity, human resources or infrastructure to effectively manage their territory and improve the well-being of their populations.

There is considerable legal ambiguity in the fiscal provisions of the decentralization process because the terms stipulated in the constitution do not always correspond to those stipulated in other new institutional codes. The 2002 Forestry Code, for example, introduces the condition that provinces retrocede 15 per cent of their revenues to decentralized entities from which resources were extracted. To date, no mechanisms have been put in place to ensure this retrocession. This ambiguity in the legal framework helps account for lack of progress in moving towards decentralization.

While decentralization could have positive implications for more accountable government for ordinary citizens at the local level, there is also the risk that it could create or reinforce sentiments of xenophobia or reinforce oppression of minorities (Marysse 2005; Weiss and Nzongola-Ntalalaja 2009). Congo has experienced repeated instances of ethnic rivalries and even ethnic cleansing in the recent past. Persecution and expulsion of ethnic Kasaians from Katanga in the 1990s is a notable example (Dibwe dia Mwemba 2006). In the current context of extreme poverty and competition over access to jobs and resources, decentralization could exacerbate insider–outsider tensions. Another possible repercussion of this could be reduced mobility for purposes of education, work or commerce from one province to another. A related risk pertains to the possible establishment of local-level tyrants. A best-case scenario of improved democratic governance at the national level would not necessarily imply greater democracy at the local level. De facto autonomy of the Kivus from Kinshasa and the presence of human rights criminals/leaders like Laurent Nkunda who 'govern' their territories according to their own rules and practices are factors that decentralization planners will have to take into account.

DRC is a diverse society with a strong sense of national identity. It is multi-ethnic, multilingual and multi-denominational. The sentiment of being Congolese is vibrant, even though people complain about government and leadership. Mobutu's 'authenticity' discourses and wars of aggression contributed to the gradual emergence of a Congolese sense of belonging. Music, sport, fashion and religion have contributed to the consolidation of a trans-ethnic national conscience. Congolese are simultaneously or alternatively Kongo, Luba, Yaka, Tetela or other ethnic groups when for reasons of social, political or economic opportunism, it is convenient to shift from one identity to another. The overlapping and multiplication of identities has helped Congolese counteract the negative effects of political oppression and economic constraints because they broaden their solidarity networks. This pragmatic overlapping is an important facet of being Congolese and extends beyond ethnicity. It embraces other kinds of identity dimensions relating to religion, profession or grassroots associations. People living in Kinshasa have a long-standing reputation of being particularly proud to belong to the social group known as Kinois. A more recent trend is the development of collective pride based on provincial identity. Decentralization could benefit from this emerging sense of provincial identity but only if it is embedded in a meaningful process of democratization that could be appropriated by ordinary Congolese.

Industrial logging and social challenges

The international community has been heavily involved in preparing Congo's economic future. The World Bank's involvement in drafting and having promulgated new mining and forestry codes is a notable illustration. The World Bank's position – shared by other major actors such as the European Union, the United States and Belgium – is that stability in DRC will be largely contingent upon improved management of the country's outstanding natural heritage. There is broad consensus that Congo's natural resources could help kick-start the formal economy. They could also be a basis for reconstruction and poverty alleviation if major changes in the political economy of the country are implemented along with increased transparency and accountability. State control over natural resources, in partnership with responsible private sector actors, could arguably contribute to sustainable peace and development. Development experts, therefore, have designed policies that seek to formalize those key sectors of the economy that have either been exploited through patrimonial practices or pillaged by foreign actors who collude with high-level corrupt elites. This situation of collusion was documented in detail by United Nations experts (United Nations Panel of Inquiry 2003, 2009). The manner in which mining and logging concessions have been awarded constitutes a serious handicap to the implementation of these policies. Given the high economic stakes, the shift from patrimonialism to transparency will require a revolution in attitudes and political behaviour.

World Bank experts argue that the DRC has to gear up its industrial forestry sector in a responsible manner. 'Responsible' here translates into protecting community and indigenous rights, respect for the environment and equitable distribution of benefits. They also see logging as one of the most important growth sectors in the coming years because of its economic potential and its potential to be formalized and controlled. It is a fundamental assumption behind rehabilitating the Congolese economy that makes sense. Embedded in this World Bank logic is the strategy of formalizing potential growth sectors of the economy so the country can continue paying back its external debt and attract foreign investments.

The World Bank's logic and actions in the DRC industrial logging sector are nonetheless subject to some criticism. First, they are a clear example of an international organization replacing the Congo state and making strategic decisions that should be the prerogatives of sovereign states. In 2002, when the Forestry Code[10] was designed, World Bank representatives occupied key posts as advisers in the relevant ministries, a situation that can be interpreted as undermining the process of state reform. Replacing the state, or acting on its behalf, does not build capacity. Secondly, they raise serious ethical questions because there is little doubt that local populations will be victimized by industrialized logging. Although the Code establishes mechanisms to make sure they are not denied access to productive and cultural space, they may suffer from depletion of vital forest products as loggers transform the ecology and social relations in what local populations consider as their ancestral lands. Thirdly, strategies proposed by the Bank reveal a certain lack of basic knowledge of the country's size and logistical handicaps, making policy implementation difficult. It also seems that Bank experts did not grasp the complexity of indigenous representation issues. Fourthly, the Bank supported the validation of concession titles (referred to as the conversion process) even though it withdrew from the zoning process (establishing country-wide land-use planning), which should have come first. These problems accentuate perceptions that the international community is imposing reform without taking into account local realities and expectations.

Approximately forty million Congolese depend on forest

resources for their daily needs. Forests provide them with wood for cooking and building, game and fish for protein and a wide range of non-timber forest products for food, healing, crafts and rituals. Given its size and ecological characteristics, DRC is one of the world's top ten mega-biodiversity countries. Although forests provide important earnings for a small group of about twenty official industrial loggers (mainly foreign), their contribution to the national economy is insignificant.[11] This can be explained by the enormous macroeconomic challenges to improved forestry management. A significant constraint is exorbitant freight and transport costs because of poor road, port and rail infrastructure. Navigation between Kisangani and Kinshasa on the Congo river is satisfactory but the rapids slightly downstream from the capital mean that goods must be loaded on trains or lorries in Kinshasa before reaching the Matadi port, increasing costs and causing serious bottlenecks because of the port's limited capacity. Other constraints include very high operating costs; political insecurity, which is a disincentive to investors, making economies of scale unattainable; an arbitrary and unpredictable tax system; and complaints by loggers that they have to replace the state with respect to provision of social services and development of infrastructure.

The potential timber production is estimated at over ten million cubic metres per year, but the annual production rate has barely reached 500,000 cubic metres, and forest revenue on average is less than 1 per cent of annual GDP. The bulk of timber exports are in the form of tree trunks: only a small percentage of Congolese timber is processed or partially processed. Moreover, a large share of timber harvesting is being carried out by either illegal loggers or small-scale informal harvesters. According to some estimates, forest revenues have increased since 2002, in part because of improved tax collection policies (Malele Mbala and Karsenty 2009). While this may be perceived as a positive sign, more revenues for the central government do not necessarily translate into direct benefits for ordinary people.

Congo has a total forest cover of 108 million hectares and half of this surface is designated as commercial forest (Devers and

Vande weghe 2006: 29). In 2009, 9 million hectares were under concession – an important reduction compared with the early 1990s, when 45 million hectares were under concession (Roda and Erdlenbruch 2003: 1; Global Witness 2009). This reduction can be explained by World Bank policies implemented by Congolese authorities aimed at revoking contracts on lands that were not generating tax revenues because they were not exploited or were under-exploited. In January 2009, an inter-ministerial commission in charge of examining logging contracts decided to cancel 91 out of 156 logging contracts under review; 65 contracts were converted into long-term concessions. In principle, only those contracts that respected strict technical, social, environmental and economic conditions stipulated in the Forest Code and in the 2005 presidential decree could be converted into forest concessions. The World Bank, moreover, was put under serious pressure from indigenous rights advocacy groups and NGOs, which also contributed to contract terminations.[12]

Given this complex context in which a wide range of stakeholders compete for access to resources, there are major disadvantages for local communities who live in and around forest concessions. These high-stake economic spaces have become conflict-ridden social spaces. This reality is exacerbated by a very ambiguous institutional framework: positive change in the forestry sector will require much more than a change of government or the elaboration of new laws and policies. International donor funding may help address some immediate problems but is unable to change deep-rooted ideologies and practices. A tripartite modus vivendi between local populations, the private sector and the Congo state is an absolute prerequisite for any form of rehabilitation of the formal economy in general and the logging sector in particular. The new legal and regulatory framework relating to logging offers some opportunities to improve the well-being of local populations in the spirit of sustainable management, but the administrative, logistical and institutional control mechanisms are non-existent or insufficient.

The 2002 Forestry Code included substantial requirements for public consultation and integration of social and environmental factors into the forest concession allocation process. In theory, this represents a significant improvement over past laws and practices because until the 2002 Code was passed, the sector was governed by a colonial decree dating back to 1949. The need to modernize legislation and practices owing to unsustainable forest management schemes was obvious and long overdue. An independent observatory was set up in 2005 to provide technical support for the conversion of old forest titles to new concessions.[13] The observatory was mandated to identify titles that were awarded illegally during the moratorium that was imposed after the UN report on the illegal exploitation of Congo's natural wealth, identify titles that had not paid surface or exploitation taxes, and ensure that all stakeholders are involved in the conversion process. A major challenge faced by the observatory was accommodating the competing claims to forests by concession holders and indigenous communities (notably Batwa Pygmy communities) that have little or no voice in decision-making debates. The real pertinence of the observatory, which mobilized a large amount of organizational energy and funding – like many such initiatives in Africa – is ambiguous. It reviewed applications for concessions based on technical, legal and social criteria but its recommendations were not binding. A Congolese inter-ministerial commission ultimately decided which applications to accept for concession awards. Oversight of the final decisions was kept to a strict minimum.

The Forest Code specifies the land and resource rights of local populations and stipulates the obligations of the concession holder to provide social services (Article 89). One of its main advantages is the attempt to narrow the gap between the theory of state power and the reality of customary law (Article 36). This is an important step forward because traditional claims are now recognized and institutionalized. Even within concessions, local populations have the right to hunt, fish and harvest non-timber forest products (Article 44). Until 2002, the state claimed sole ownership of land and resources. The 1949 law that governed forestry issues until 2002 institutionalized the absence of any indigenous claims or rights. If loggers previously set up schools, clinics and company stores or organized clubhouses with satellite TV or other such initiatives, it was because they sought to maintain a minimum level of social peace (*acheter la paix sociale* in the words of local people). They had absolutely no legal obligation to do so. It was largely owing to the involvement of indigenous peoples' lobbies and environmental NGOs that the 2002 Code recognized the importance of working with local populations with respect to forest management.

In practice, however, industrial loggers are reluctant to invest in social infrastructure because they claim that the taxes they pay to the central government should cover those responsibilities. They further argue that it is incumbent on the state to respect its responsibilities. As a response to this reluctance, a presidential decree was promulgated on 24 October 2005 requiring loggers to make concrete propositions in their management plans (*plans de relance*) to protect local populations' rights and practices (*les droits d'usage*). In the spirit of participatory management (consultative committees are institutionalized in Article 29 of the Forestry Code), these propositions must be supported by signed reports of meetings held between loggers and representatives of local communities. The decree has similar requirements with respect to the environmental impacts of industrial logging (threats to wildlife, for example) and the implications that these impacts could have on the well-being of communities.

Despite these requirements, land tenure practices still remain riddled with ambiguities. Badly needed land reform has not been seriously addressed. Traditional authorities and state agents vie for power, access to resources and legitimacy in an unending negotiation process characterized by turf wars and hard bargaining in and around logging concessions. Civil society actors such as religious figures, NGO workers and international development experts have become omnipresent. They are not, however, very effective actors. Relations between these actors are conflictual, even though a situation of fragile accommodation has been worked out. According to the DRC government, land (literally *le sol et le sous-sol*) belongs to the state. The 1966 Bakajika Law enabled the state to claim full sovereignty over land issues, including the awarding of agricultural, forest and mining concessions. The other, opposing, logic is the one maintained by the people living in rural communities. They consider themselves to be the real landowners based on ancestral rights. They claim to be the guardians of the land, making the cosmic link between their ancestors and future generations. The Bakajika Law for them is no more than illegitimate fiction invented in Kinshasa for political reasons. The potential for conflict in and around forest concessions results from this hybrid system, which is exacerbated by the ambiguity that surrounds procedures and their implementation. There is no clearly defined set of rules in these spaces because in the context of state failure and economic crisis whoever has the slightest degree of power or authority exploits it to maximize his own personal gains. Taking the claims and preoccupations of forest communities into account is a positive sign but there is considerable room for scepticism with respect to the capacity of administrations to uphold the law – especially in a sector where corrupt practices at the highest levels remain commonplace. For the time being, relevant ministries are unable to guarantee that these laws and procedures are enforced.

The constitution stipulates that 60 per cent of revenues are destined for the central government and 40 per cent for the twenty-six provinces. The provinces in turn retrocede 15 per cent to those smaller administrative districts called *secteurs* from where revenues are generated. Concretely, this means that if a logging company pays $100,000 in tax to Kinshasa, $15,000 will be earmarked for the *secteur* in which the timber was harvested. In 2010, the governor of timber-rich Equateur province tried to ban logging activities as a way of putting pressure on Kinshasa to respect its financial decentralization commitments.[14] Given the economic stakes and the relations that exist between concession holders and political elites in Kinshasa, he was unsuccessful. Territorial agents who should logically be involved in financial transfers are marginalized. In addition to overwhelming political obstacles, they stressed a range of logistical problems in receiving funds from higher administrative echelons. Congo is a country with practically no formal banking system and ministries that are only just now starting to use computers. Administrators in rural areas sometimes have bicycles but rarely have vehicles to travel in their districts. Another unsolved problem pertains to who exactly within the community should receive this 15 per cent, in what form and for what specific purposes. There is insufficient harmony at the village level to imagine that people can reach a consensus on how to distribute or invest new revenues. This is especially problematic in communities that live largely outside of a cash economy because power structures in rural Congo institutionalize a certain number of exclusions.

Power is controlled by Bantu men, the elders, who alone decide how the community should preserve its past and organize its future. Women have no voice. Pygmies have no voice. In the forest areas of DRC, Pygmy communities – widely considered as being 'backward' – are numerically significant. Although some progress has been made at the discourse level, this has had practically no impact on the lived realities of women and indigenous peoples. These exclusions are serious handicaps to the Congo's broader development needs. There are many examples of conflicts that have arisen within communities because members do not always share the same views about how to deal with the presence of loggers in their areas. Even the seemingly positive question of socio-economic investment creates conflicts over choice of location and choice of development initiative: some people may want a school, others may want a bridge, and still others may want a well or water pump. Logging companies reinforce these forms of exclusion because their interlocutors are the Bantu male elders who make decisions in non-participatory ways. Policies should therefore take into account (in addition to local logics and belief systems) the host of cleavages, tensions, problems of distrust, and gender and generation gaps that haunt forest communities.

This analysis of the logging sector challenges the view that new policies can contribute to poverty alleviation or improved well-being. While people are integral elements of tropical forest ecosystems and need to be consulted, informed and involved when elaborating national priority policies such as concession awards, the mechanisms currently in place in DRC are woefully insufficient. These populations tend to be uninformed of their rights. They lack experience in participatory strategies and have few reliable civil society mediators. Participation is hampered by a host of obstacles ranging from the complex nature of traditional authority and its institutionalization of inequality to the long-established practices of high-level corruption in the logging sector. The participatory management approach that is fashionable in some donor and NGO circles has little currency in the ruthless world of industrial logging.

This bleak analysis of Congo's forestry sector confirms that reform initiatives are tantamount to masquerade. Can new ideas and policies pertaining to socially and ecologically sustainable forest management really work? There is little evidence that proves this so in the Congo. Sustainable forestry is not a technical challenge: it is a political, social and cultural problem. Can Congolese authorities responsible for forest management design and implement locally appropriate policies that will enable the country as a whole to benefit from logging revues? Again, there is little evidence that proves so.

4 | The administrative juggernaut

The administrative reform flaw

A fundamental error in the overall reform process is the expected involvement of Congolese administrative services. Implementation of reform policies depends on the commitment and effectiveness of a competent, honest and motivated cadre of civil servants. But after decades of state collapse, Congo's public service sector is unable to cope with even minimal service provision – and even less with contributing to or managing reform. Administrative reform is an externally driven objective that has not taken Congolese work practices and ethics into consideration. These latter are largely incompatible with Western perceptions and operational logic. Ordinary Congolese have lost respect for civil servants, whom they see as predators, not service providers. Most civil servants have not absorbed the need for reform and have succeeded in resisting change. International efforts aimed at transforming Congolese administrations have been largely unsuccessful, essentially for the same reasons that explain failure in other reform efforts.

'The state is dying but not dead ... State agents are so present, but so useless ... The state doesn't do anything for us ... Instead of the state taking care of the people, we cater to civil servants and do the state's work. Things were much better before.' These expressions, which combine nostalgia and legitimate complaints, sum up the perception ordinary Congolese have of the state and state agents. They are commonly heard refrains throughout the country, inexorably expressed in all of the country's languages by the poor and the well-to-do. Nevertheless, the administration and its representatives remain unavoidable forces in Congo's social, economic, political and cultural and arenas. The term 'juggernaut'

Four

is appropriate here because it refers to an unstoppable force with crushing power. But why is the state still so powerful and omnipresent in the daily lives of these people wronged by colonial oppression, dictatorship and economic underdevelopment? How can this paradox be explained? How, concretely, does the state manifest itself and who are its agents? Does the *raison d'être* of the Congolese state go beyond the violence of exploitation and predation? This chapter will respond to these questions. It will also provide an overview of administrative reform strategies proposed by Congo's international partners in recent years.

Analysis of Congolese public administration is the approach adopted here. It emphasizes the relations between people and public services.[1] This is pertinent because workers, students, the unemployed, people from the formal and informal sectors, housewives and street vendors throughout the country are all condemned to deal with the hungry representatives of public administrations. Escaping them is impossible. Avoiding a tax – be it official or arbitrarily invented on the spot – is a daunting challenge for some and a daily exercise for others. While most people do whatever they can to outwit the state agent in front of them, the latter relies on a host of tactics and strategies to have the final word. As arbitrariness reigns supreme, state agents try to ante up the fine, tax or fee. Meanwhile, people try to pay the smallest amount possible. At the outcome of *palabre* (the ritual negotiation process), each party usually ends up with something: compromise is generally preferred to a unilateral decision. Beyond monetary loss or gain, saving face is also an important consideration.

The presence of state agents and the institutionalization of negotiation processes and scenarios for all kinds of exchange remind people of the stubborn persistence of the state. Although the administrative machine is clearly more manifest in towns and cities, rural populations (which comprise approximately half of the Congolese population) are also within its reach. State crisis in Congo is characterized by loss of legitimacy, abdication from the development agenda, incapacity to maintain the monopoly of coercion, shortcomings in the management of political and technical priorities and the inability to mobilize, generate or manage internal and external financial resources. Despite these overwhelming problems, the Congo endures as an administrative space in which state agents and citizens seem to have reached a complex but workable form of accommodation. Congolese have a bizarre love-hate relationship with the state and its administrative machine, notwithstanding its brutality and corrupt practices at all levels. This analysis consequently puts into perspective the frequently expressed idea of a non-existent state.

Why the administration persists

Even though state crisis certainly handicaps the modus oper-andi of state services, it has hardly made them disappear. They still clearly have a *raison d'être* throughout society, for elites and ordinary citizens alike. State crisis has, however, significantly transformed the original mandates of these services. The adminis-tration is a powerful machine that contributes to the perpetuation and reproduction of the state as a sovereign political and territorial entity. Although a recent World Bank report on governance in DRC makes reference to 'the administration's endurance and a few pockets of functionality', it also argues that the administra-tion 'seems to have abandoned its original objectives' (World Bank 2005: iii). In a study devoted specifically to the endurance of the Congo state and Congolese nationalism, Pierre Englebert highlights the Congo state's 'stunning propensity for resilience' (2003: 2), despite all the indicators that suggest total state collapse. He also suggests that '... weak African states endure because they have engineered legitimacy for themselves over time, irrespective of their lack of capacity' (Englebert 2009: 54). These pertinent depictions are borrowed here to explain the resiliency of the Congolese administration.

Exploitation and predation are the dominant explanations accounting for the persistence of the Congolese state in gen-eral, and the administration in particular (Rackley 2006; Mbaya and Streiffeler 1999: 11). Mobutu instructed civil servants and soldiers to 'feed off the population' (*population baza bilanga ya bino*). While discourses have mutated because of good governance initiatives, practices have not evolved. In the war-torn areas of eastern Congo, soldiers and militia have taken this relationship to extremes, claiming that 'with a gun you can eat', or 'your gun is your salary'. These forms of predation thrive in environments where there is no oversight or accountability.

Another interpretation contrasting normative concepts of good governance and real practices of governance is put forward by Giorgio Blundo (for West African states): 'Participation, decentralization and administrative transparency need to be interpreted as being particular governmental technologies endowed with their own political rationalities and "governmentalities"' (2002: 3). A further useful explanation is expressed by Dominique Darbon: 'the relationship between service providers and service users is based on uncertainty and discrimination, resulting in a culture of fear, evasion and periodic predation when the opportunity arises' (2002: 85). He also underscores the importance of addressing administrative reform in the specific social and political environments of beneficiary countries, which is a cogent recommendation for the process in DRC (Darbon 2003).

Three reasons account for the persistence of the administration in Congo. First, the administration is instrumentalized by the state's political elites. They exploit it in the same way they exploit mafia-type networks for political survival and personal enrichment. Even though they exploit and manipulate these networks, they are at the same time dependent on them. The administrative machine in place today in Congo is a tenacious colonial legacy. Despite the flagrant contradictions and internecine haggling that characterize the symbiosis between state and administration, one could not exist without the other. Aloko Gbodu Ombeng already observed this situation more than twenty years ago in his study of Zairean civil servants. He described the phenomenon as being one of 'fusion and confusion' between state and administrative bodies (1987/88: 232).

Instrumentalization is a dynamic and constant process, notably for strategic reasons. The state manifests itself via the administration for security purposes, for example, which is one of its fundamental sovereign prerogatives. The branches involved in the protection of territory and population – but especially protection of the elites themselves – are the army, the police, the intelligence services (Agence nationale de renseignement – ANR) and border control (Direction générale des migrations – DGM). Although the Ministry of Defence and the Ministry of the Interior theoretically control these services, important decisions emanate directly from President Joseph Kabila and his advisers. In this context, the administration is instrumentalized to reinforce and stabilize political elites. This can also be interpreted as being the deliberate production of 'clever power' opposed to the production of 'weak power' (Diouf 2002: 33). This refers to the advantages that political elites derive from seemingly unmanageable political situations that they in fact help produce and perpetuate.

The state also wields considerable control in the strategic financial arena. Internally, priority is given to services that generate public revenues such as the Direction générale des impôts, the Office des douanes et accises (OFIDA), the Direction générale de recettes administratives, domaniales et judiciaires (DGRAD) and the Office congolais de contrôle (OCC). The high-level officials who manage these services are not selected haphazardly; their appointments are decided at the top of the political pyramid and respect clearly defined paternalistic logic and patron–client patterns. At the external financial level, the state manifests itself via the administration in the framework of development cooperation by channelling the funds of the international community.

Even though these institutions rely on a corps of international experts and consultants, the involvement of Congolese civil servants is unavoidable: less so for the identification and definition of projects and programmes but certainly for their implementation. In the context of 'recolonization' of the Congo, the state maintains some degree of control through this strategy. The role of Congolese civil servants is also crucial for the implementation of humanitarian operations or NGO initiatives in the areas of health, education and infrastructure. Without their support, the success of these actions could be seriously handicapped or even sabotaged if an official, however petty, is not sufficiently 'motivated' to deal with a file or have a document signed by a supervisor.

The personal survival of its staff is the second reason accounting for the persistence of the administration. Civil servants and other state agents have privatized what is officially public service provision. This privatization helps explain why official salaries account for only between 5 and 10 per cent of earnings (Verheijen 2008: 21). Ambiguous and non-transparent bonuses, indemnities and cash (in the form of extortion money, bribes and kickbacks) paid by service users constitute the bulk of monthly earnings. This transformation is conditioned by the ways administrative personnel cleverly exploit the advantages associated with their status or their occupation of positions of authority. They constantly invent new tricks and schemes that could be qualified as 'social cannibalism' in a context where society is its own self-consuming prey. Relations between civil servants (people) and the administrative services (the structure) are embedded in a complex and interdependent framework. Without the structure, agents have no reason to exist. Conversely, without staff, these services would cease to function. The survival of agents thus depends on the perpetuation of the administrative structure. Agents consequently need to justify the importance of their work – and themselves – by rendering services that are often insignificant, such as issuing authorizations, certificates and testimonials and by wielding the stamps and seals of their power.

The value of these symbols is an important but often underestimated political reality. It is in this sense that administrative procedures continue to contribute to identity formation in Congo today. Without these symbols – a voter registration card, for example – one can easily cease to exist in the eyes of the administration. Service users consequently attach considerable importance to this dimension of what is clearly unavoidable administrative reality. This situation, moreover, helps put into perspective many of the negative stereotypes so frequently expressed about the

Congo. Authorities at all levels have succeeded in maintaining the real and imagined value of these symbols. They manipulate discourses on the power of symbols and the symbols of power, sometimes with finesse but sometimes with brutality. A retired railway worker from Lubumbashi, for example, highlighted this by declaring: 'documents pertaining to my meagre pension are crucial for my survival, they are my life' (Trefon with Ngoy 2007: 92). For civil servants, the administration – and of course its peripheral economic buffer zone – is not something to be taken lightly. The administration and the state, for them and their families, are not an empty shell but a vital reality.

Persistence of the administration can also be explained by the volume and the diversity of services sought by the population. This pertains mainly to real services that are addressed in non-conventional ways. Certain services require specific administrative or technical actions that the state alone is able to fulfil. Given their necessity, people reinforce the state in these areas, helping it to reproduce itself. To avoid public schools closing their doors, for example, parents participate in 'motivating' teachers by paying them bonuses to supplement the salaries they receive from the state. These teachers are part of the administration that recruits them and awards diplomas. Despite the crisis of the public school system, having at least one high school graduate in the family with a state diploma (*le diplôme d'Etat*) continues to be a powerful objective for Congolese parents. A similar example is given by a Lubumbashi market woman. Instead of simply contacting the national electricity provider (Société nationale d'électricité – SNEL) and expecting them to connect her house with electric power, she explains how the neighbourhood had to form an association, identify a group leader, collect money, buy the electric cables and other material, and finally negotiate with the SNEL workers and pay them for the technical and administrative work they eventually performed (ibid.: 109). This is a typical example of new forms of state–society relations in the DRC: an ephemeral neighbourhood association cooperating directly with a national agency to obtain a concrete result. The population benefits because they get electricity at home (except, of course, during the frequent blackout periods) and the SNEL agents benefit because they are paid hard cash for their expertise in addition to their inadequate and randomly paid state salaries. This type of semi-public, semi-private hybrid solution is characteristic of relations between people and the state in many areas of public life in the Congo.

Disillusioned personnel

State agents in Congo have every reason to be disillusioned given the degradation of their working conditions over the past twenty years. First, salaries quite simply do not cover basic needs. The average civil servant's monthly wage is less than $50. Buying food, paying rent, school fees, transportation and other expenses is difficult for families because these expenditures tend to be more than ten times the official average monthly salary. Legal social advantages are not respected either. When the economy was still relatively solid in the 1960s and 1970s, civil servants received instalment allowances upon being hired, marriage gifts, salary advances in justifiable cases, funeral costs for family members, holiday bonuses and regular cost-of-living increases. Today, these perks are only memories. This situation explains why people say they live 'thanks to miracles' or 'by the grace of God'. It also explains why civil servants have to play more than one card at a time to make ends meet.

The working environment is another source of frustration. Four to eight people gather around a few tables on uncomfortable chairs in an office, sometimes without electric lighting. The toilets that were installed decades ago are more likely than not blocked up today. An old minivan behind the Lubumbashi courthouse recently served as a toilet for staff. Whatever office furniture and equipment there may be is old and dilapidated. Few civil servants have computers and practically none have landline telephones. Sometimes, however, the clackety-clack of an old mechanical type-writer can be heard. To make a phone call, civil servants have to use their own mobile phone credits. The emergence of the cybercafé, where people can make phone calls, use computers, access the Internet and pay for secretarial services, is a partial solution for civil servants. It is obviously the service user (who is perceived as a client or as prey) who ultimately pays whatever costs have been incurred, constituting another example of the privatization of public services.

Archives and other documents that have resisted termites are piled up on the floor, given the absence of filing cabinets and shelves. Another problem with archives is the fact that civil servants often consider themselves the alpha and omega of their services. Studies, reports and other archival elements are perceived as being either useless or dangerous and are removed or destroyed when a civil servant takes on new responsibilities – if they have not already been disposed of by his predecessor. This behaviour is contrary to the very logic of the administration, which is mandated to assure continuity in policies and procedures.

Lack of motivation is also associated with medical services for workers and their families. In the past, again, they received free healthcare. Today, public medical facilities are unable to offer meaningful or trustworthy care. Left to fend for themselves, public servants are likewise worried about how they will cope upon retirement. The 'golden age' is widely perceived as a looming nightmare. Based on what they learn from their predecessors, those that have no family to depend upon fear they will either become beggars or die prematurely. This social dilemma was addressed by the World Bank with a view to streamlining public service, retiring civil servants who have exceeded the legal retirement age and redefining recruitment strategies, but implementation was unsuccessful, in part because of the capacity of civil servants to resist change. In 2005, the World Bank paid $47 million in the form of direct budgetary support to a project to retire 100,000 civil servants. As this was right in the middle of the electoral process, the money was reallocated by the government. Only $4 million was devoted to the original project.[2] This is an excellent illustration of public development aid gone wrong and appropriation of public funds for political advantage.

The negative image of the *fonctionnaire* in the eyes of service users is yet another problem. Considered as social parasites, they incarnate pettiness and misery – especially those who are at the bottom of the administrative hierarchy. They are the embodiment of a failed state. Prior to the economic crisis, who was not jealous of them? In the late colonial period, joining the ranks of the Administration d'Afrique was a prestigious step for Congolese. The deterioration of the image of the civil service and the gradual process of state collapse took place at the same time. Today, accusing someone of 'wearing the jacket of state agent' is a cruel insult.

Public service providers in Congo have been forced to prioritize personal gain. Discipline or loyalty to their duties is secondary. The conditions, steps and requirements necessary to obtain a single administrative document, for example, have been carefully redefined to allow the entire administrative hierarchy to benefit in one way or another. If someone dares ask for a receipt, the usual reply is 'Who is going to pay for the receipt booklet?' Formality and informality thus emerge as the recto and verso of public service. They are the two facets of the same random state. This duality has also been expressed as pragmatism versus conformity (Delta I Consulting 2002: 17) and as social logic versus administrative imperatives (Mpinga 1970: 304). This situation, which makes a Weberian system of service delivery unrealistic, lends credibility to the argument articulated by Chabal and Daloz: 'informalization is nothing other than the day-to-day instrumentalization of what is a shifting and ill-defined political realm' (1999: 149).

The civil service recruitment process is also a good example of the negotiated and ambiguous character of the Congolese administration. Although the official procedure calls for a selection process based on merit and transparency to allow for equal opportunities, discretion governs how individuals are hired. Recruitment criteria are nebulous and hidden from the general public. Information is transmitted by word of mouth and within closed networks, ethnic circles and other forms of patron–client relationships. A World Bank report euphemistically confirms this:

'recruitment is carried out in a haphazard way (without consider-ing the availability of budget resources)', and adds: 'the Public Service Ministry has effectively been marginalized and has been unable to enforce across the board standards' (Verheijen and Mabi 2008: 2).

The decision to hire an agent for service anywhere in the country necessarily emanates from the administrative hierarchy in Kinshasa, which alone has the authority to issue a badge number (*numéro de matricule*). Local authorities, nonetheless, do have some leeway to support their candidate. This set of procedures creates an ambiguous work environment because, while agents take orders from the local provincial or municipal chain of com-mand, they must also respect injunctions emanating from the distant capital. The statute of the civil servant is consequently incompatible with the logic of territorial decentralization. The incompatibility results from de facto territorial decentralization not being accompanied by the decentralization of public service, which is still centralized. Civil servants are consequently subject to two parallel forms of command. One implication of this pluralism is the increased capacity of civil servants to exploit their positions of authority to satisfy their own needs.

Attitudes and daily practices of civil servants in this context are geared more to the fulfilment of personal expectations than the execution of public service. This Congolese reality helps account for a host of administrative weaknesses such as absenteeism, strategic foot-dragging, featherbedding, collusion, obstruction of justice, private payment for public service, destruction or accid-ental loss of archives and other forms of petty corruption. State agents have all but abandoned the principles of continuity of services and equality of users. Services, the time devoted to an individual, justice or other rights all accrue to the highest bidder; namely, those who have efficient intermediaries, friends in high places or strong bargaining capacity.

The work ethic of civil servants is less an issue of professional loyalty than one of personal survival and improving the lot of their families. This has an impact on the amount of time a civil servant is present at work. Human resource management in Congolese administrations is generally of poor quality. Refresher courses and other forms of continuing education are rare and there is little concern for institutionalized career planning. Many civil servants consequently moonlight by running small shops and offering services. Others combine public service with urban or peri-urban agriculture. This class of civil servants has adopted as a motto 'help yourself first', transforming President Mobutu's famously cynical slogan 'help – don't help yourself' (*servir et non se servir*).

This bleak portrait contrasts sharply with the huge benefits that some civil servants generate from their positions. While the majority find it more logical to tend to their small farm plots instead of going to the office, others are highly motivated to go to work. The head accountant at the town hall or the tax controllers from OFIDA (Customs and Excise Tax Service), for example, can hardly afford to miss a day's work given their capacity to waylay ordinary citizens. A similar case is that of the civil servant responsible for issuing vaccination cards and health certificates in the public health department for the city of Lubumbashi (Dibwe dia Mwemba 2002: 49). Despite the tendency to denigrate public service today in Congo, it is precisely because of these petty fiefdoms that people are still interested in being recruited into the administration. Access to these positions is based on nepotism, a recommendation by an elite and other forms of patron–client relations. Merit is not a factor that carries much weight in the selection process. In order for officials to remain in these 'juicy' positions, a percentage of the benefits must trickle upwards. If not, an official would be quickly replaced by someone else more respectful of this golden rule of patron–client relations. This also explains why ordinary Congolese complain of being between the hammer and anvil of the administration.

Ambiguity, randomness and negotiation

The Congolese public administration is ambiguous, arbitrary and hybrid. Negotiation with its agents is constant. Administrative procedures are conditioned by the mood, availability and the personal expectations and needs of civil servants. Depending on the context, they may adopt a formal discourse (strictly adhering to rules and regulations), just as they may opt for an informal approach (inventing or 'interpreting' rules). From a strictly formal perspective, the administration is based on legal instruments that define state–society relations, specifying rights and responsibilities. Theoretically, the Congolese administration defines how the population is controlled, maintains census data and ensures its well-being. It is mandated to prepare budget forecasts and collect the state's taxes. Municipal administrations in DRC are responsible for public order, the economy, public works, agriculture and animal husbandry, environmental management and cultural issues. These services frame the legal context in which state agents manoeuvre and jockey for superiority. They remind users of this legal framework to intimidate them during the inescapable negotiation processes that govern their relations. While most political science research over the past twenty years has focused nearly exclusively on informal power relations, bringing back the formal administrative context is an important means to help understand the dynamics of contemporary African state issues.

Ambiguity is exacerbated by impunity for irregularities and abuses. The predatory strategies of state agents are explicitly approved by hierarchal bosses because they directly benefit from the proceeds exacted by their subalterns. Congolese are all too frequently reminded of the expression: 'you won't get any satisfaction by complaining about the crocodile to the hippopotamus because they both live in the same murky water'. Kahola reported an example of this in a Lubumbashi police station. Policemen justify beating inmates unless they give them money by arguing that if they do not do so, their children will go hungry (2006: 29). Abuse results from the absence of recourse to a higher body interested in sanctioning such treatment. State agents (or impostors) rarely have uniforms, badges or other forms of insignia that allow people to identify who these sometimes real, sometimes false agents truly are. This also facilitates the harassment of service users.

Negotiation is the common theme running through state–society relations in Congo. Exchanges between service providers and service users are all based on some form of negotiation. Congolese invariably complain of hassles, intimidation and vulnerability. They allude to arbitration, intercession (the importance of using the services or talents of a go-between) and social proximity (seeking help from a friend of a friend). Every administrative situation, problem or request has an appropriate series of steps to be followed. The mechanisms of this process are coded and assimilated by stakeholders. Negotiation is omnipresent at all levels, irrespective of the stakes. People quibble over the price of a bag of cooking charcoal, just as a well-to-do wholesaler haggles over the amount of money he will pay as annual income tax.

One of the golden rules that service users have been forced to accept is conjugation of the verb 'to eat' in the first person plural. 'We eat' works; 'I eat' does not. Those who try eating alone, without sharing with civil servants, are sure to have problems. Conjugating the verb in the present tense, 'we eat', is also more likely to avoid hassles because promises of sharing in the future, 'we shall eat', are clearly less acceptable. The importance of gift-giving is obvious: tips, motivation and car fare are a few euphemisms – along with numerous eating metaphors exemplified by Bayart (1993). These code words confirm the entrenched practice of selling public services for private benefit.

Despite the hassles that invariably accompany the administrative itineraries of ordinary Congolese, they do not overreact to them. The relative absence of serious conflict is rather surprising. Hassles are strategically orchestrated by state agents to prepare for a mutually satisfactory denouement. An extreme case is recourse to a 'Stockholm syndrome'-type strategy. After ill-treating a service user, a civil servant agrees to take him under his protection to avoid worse problems with his predatory colleagues. The unfortunate service user can hardly refuse this 'protection' or the ransom demanded.

All of these different forms of negotiation thrive in the arbitrary context of the Congolese state system. Formality and informality are intertwined: the discretionary application of rules depends on the needs and expectations of the agent and the financial or social position of the citizen. This arbitrary violence has been described as the embeddedness of corruptive practices within post-colonial African society (Blundo and Olivier de Sardan 2001: 21).

Beyond the disorder associated with Congolese institutions, people know what they have to do to maximize gains and minimize losses. It is rare that one party wins all and the other loses all. Generally, a compromise solution is reached. The foremost premise of conflict prevention, 'never underestimate the value of a relationship', is strictly applied. All the ramifications of these negotiation processes confirm a threefold Congolese reality: a weak state, a high degree of sophistication with respect to deviance in administrative affairs, and the application of a case-by-case approach (as opposed to the application of universal rights for all). This triple reality reflects the breach between the original mandate of the post-colonial administration and the way it continues to reinvent itself according to its own logic.

Struggling to reform the unreformable

Public administrations in most countries are subordinate to the state. Political authorities define policies that are to be implemented by the administration. Even in developed democracies, this relationship is often put to the test: in Congo, it is pure fiction. Administrative personnel in Congo define their own strategies without necessarily taking into account political injunctions. Strategies have replaced policy. Administrative personnel have nonetheless elaborated dynamic forms of accommodation with both political authorities and the people. In both cases, they pragmatically address their own needs and expectations before those of the services they are supposed to provide. In some cases, they execute decisions emanating from political authorities to the letter, sometimes partially, but generally not at all. The only certainty is that personal opportunism governs their actions. It is for this reason that administrative service providers in Congo are perceived as unmanageable, undisciplined, mercenary, corrupt ...

and, quite simply, useless. A survey on how Congolese perceive the state included the question: 'If the state were a person, what would you do to him?' 'Kill him' was the unequivocal reaction of most respondents (World Bank 2005: 22). It is also for this reason that efforts are devoted to restructuring the administration in the Congo.

Administrative reform has been on the political agenda in Congo since independence. It was also an intractable problem that preoccupied Belgium during the colonial period. The size of the country, its intricate ethnic mosaic, its ecological disparity and the complex nature of the country's political economy seriously undermine its administrative organization. No sector of public life – justice, education, economy and finance, infrastructure, territorial administration and civil service – has been spared. Administrative reform was also on the agenda at the National Sovereign Conference in 1993, but the resolutions agreed upon were never implemented. Today, people believe that a less corrupt and more efficient administration is possible despite the overwhelming political challenges that need to be resolved before this drastic change could become reality.

Public administration reform in Congo entered a new phase in 2002 when the United Nations Development Programme (UNDP) launched a series of studies and consultations. The current thinking about reform reproduced the kind of efforts carried out elsewhere in Africa, again falling into the trap of the imported template approach. In the first phase (2003–06) goals included civil service capacity-building, improving human resource management, improving working conditions and promoting good governance and a professional work ethic. Expected results included recruiting civil servants on the basis of their qualifications as opposed to recruitment based on nepotism and patron–client relations, paying them decent salaries and evenly distributing human, financial and material resources between the centre (Kinshasa) and the periphery (the decentralized administrative entities). To succeed, a number of prerequisites would have to be met: revision of the legal framework of civil servants, census-taking to ascertain how many civil servants are employed by the state and establish how much they earn, provision of badly needed equipment, furniture and office supplies, tackling corruption and redefinition of the administrative organizational chart. While the logic is sound, the enabling conditions were not met. As results were extremely limited in this first phase, the second phase (ongoing since 2007) reproduced the same objectives, although some fine-tuning was introduced.

Active from 2003 to 2008, the Belgian Technical Cooperation was the main partner in administrative reform efforts. It supported reform steering committees and operational structures; provided institutional support to the Ministry of Health and the Ministry of Agriculture; supported the census operation; participated in curriculum design for the future National Institute of Administration; participated in awareness campaigns about administrative reform and the code of conduct; assisted with the revision of the legal framework; and funded numerous workshops and seminars for high-ranking civil servants. UNDP was also an important actor. It elaborated the Strategic Framework document for civil service reform; elaborated new statutes and a system for social protection; carried out studies with a view to setting up the National Institute of Administration; participated in awareness campaigns about administrative reform and the code of conduct; worked to improve human resource management; and carried out studies on how to set up a forum for social dialogue. The World Bank was also involved, mainly with a scheme to retire civil servants who had reached retirement age and arrange for a pension system. France proposed an updated payroll system, participated in capacity-building and supported the National Institute of Administration project. The fundamental census-taking project and providing software for human resource management were South Africa's contribution to the process.

In the spirit of local appropriation of the work being carried out by these partners, a number of Congolese structures were set up to harmonize, coordinate and oversee. The Comité technique de la réforme de l'administration publique (CTRAP) was set up to deal with the technical aspects of the reform; the Commission interministérielle de pilotage de la réforme des administrations publiques (CIPRAP) is an inter-ministerial initiative designed to harmonize projects within different ministries and deal with the swarm of experts and consultants subcontracted to implement actions and studies; the Secrétariat national de renforcement des capacités (SENAREC) is responsible for civil service capacity-building; the Groupe projet du Ministère de la fonction publique (GPFP) has an overseeing mandate. The creation of these different structures led to the exact opposite of what was intended. They did not communicate between themselves, coordination meetings were rarely organized and were poorly attended, responsibilities were passed on from one structure to another, and they succeeded in manipulating and creating cleavages between international partners.

How many civil servants are there exactly in the DRC? Despite efforts to find an answer to this basic question, no one knows for sure. As a first census carried out in 2005 was inconclusive, a new biometric census was launched in 2009 (but is still not finished). The process has been chaotic because some surveys are done by province while others are done by ministry. Estimates remain vague. The Central Public Service Ministry (Ministère de la fonction publique) employs approximately 130,000 staff (Verheijen and Mabi Mulumba 2008: 11).[3] This represents approximately 20 to 25 per cent of all civil servants because it does not include schoolteachers, medical staff or security forces. International partners are anxious to clarify the problem of who actually works in the public service sector because of its general implications for state-building, but also for more specific reasons pertaining to the management of budgetary support and improving payroll procedures. Chaos and ambiguity, however, are deliberately perpetuated by high-ranking civil servants. 'Fictitious agents', 'phantoms' and 'invisible agents' refer to people who may exist but do not work or may have retired or died. They allow some people in the administrative machine to embezzle funds earmarked for their salaries.

Professional evaluations have been carried out to assess progress in public administration reform (Saint-Martin 2008; Marchal et al. 2007) and a doctoral dissertation on the same subject was recently defended (Iyaka 2010). They relate cogent accounts of reform failure that apply specifically to administrative reform but also pinpoint weakness in the broader reform patchwork: the structures targeted for reform are so weak and so disorganized that reforming them is practically impossible; donor bureaucracy and procedures are major obstacles; coordination and partner synergies exist more in theory than in practice; and the DRC government has not allocated funds to contribute to reform initiatives. Absence of political leadership and appropriation is indeed an overriding handicap. Further concrete proof of this is the government's unwillingness to validate recommendations and decisions taken about administrative reform (Marchal et al. 2007: 38). This calls into question the very pertinence of the donor-driven administrative reform agenda. In a bold but relatively realistic commentary on why administrative reform has not taken root, Saint-Martin argues that it cannot be limited to the setting up of legal frameworks, redrafting rules and regulations, and designing new organizational charts and work plans, which are manageable technical issues. To be effective, reform has to confront head-on the tradition of fend-for-yourself values and culture and revolutionize mentalities (Saint-Martin 2008: 22). These problems explain the withdrawal of international partners from the administrative reform process. They have come to realize that without appropriation by the government and by the civil service agents themselves, their efforts are condemned to fail. This is why they have shifted their efforts to sectors (such as health, education and agriculture) where aid can claim to be more efficient and visible.

Attempts at administrative reform have also failed because of the absence of adequate sociological feasibility studies and because they are not based on locally appropriate world views. Insufficient effort has been made to try to define the type of administration that corresponds most closely to the needs of the Congolese.[4] Moreover, good governance initiatives, including efforts to combat corruption (designed in Washington, Paris or Brussels – and increasingly London), erroneously consider problems of Congolese service delivery more as technical problems rather than political ones (Anderson 2005; International Crisis Group 2006). Scepticism expressed about Mobutu's relations with administrative reform remains pertinent and timely today: reforms tend to be strategic positioning rather than real changes in the redistribution of power (de Saint Moulin 1988: 221).

5 | Culture matters

Insiders and outsiders

Who are political insiders and outsiders – the powerful and the powerless – and what delineates inclusion and exclusion? How do solidarity systems influence people's relations with the state? How do political repression, (dis)information, corruption and predation undermine reform initiatives? Addressing these matters in a policy-oriented perspective is an exercise that may be helpful in avoiding future pitfalls in the reform process because technocratic top-down strategies cannot be viable without paying some attention to political culture.

Congo's cultural context helps account for why reform initiatives have not achieved expected results. Culture is not necessarily the dominant explanation but it is a factor that contributes to understanding the challenges inherent in inducing political and institutional change. History and tradition are elements of the cultural reality that influence contemporary politics. This chapter advocates the need to give greater attention to attitudes and behaviours when conceptualizing initiatives for reform and state-building. Instead of attempting to defend the hypothesis that African or Congolese culture is incompatible with Western perceptions of development, democracy and modern bureaucracy, it focuses on some entrenched patterns of Congolese cultural specificity. Analysis here takes a middle ground between an essentially culturalist approach (Schatzberg 2001, 1988; Chabal and Daloz 2006) and the 'real governance' and 'practical norms' approach that emphasizes informal rules of the game based on opportunism (Olivier de Sardan 2008; Blundo and Olivier de Sardan 2001).

Political culture is one facet of the broader cultural environment and refers to 'the processes whereby political actors both understand and exploit their culture for their own ends' (Chabal and Daloz 2006: 135). Political culture is a difficult concept to harmonize with reform logics. Even well-intentioned and competent international experts working for reform tend to neglect how culture, alternatively referred to as 'the human factor', can facilitate or impede the ambitious process of social engineering being attempted in Congo today. Integrating this cultural dimension into the development agenda is a useful step in empowering communities so they can achieve independence and engage in assertive citizenship (Verhelst with Tyndale 2002: 7). It is also useful because Congolese political actors sometimes operate 'in a world with a substantially different understanding of causality and causal forces than most Western social and political scientists possess' (Schatzberg 2001: 134).

While culture may be omnipresent, often as vacuous stereotypes (Dunn 2003), drawing on cultural reality to accompany and facilitate reform is woefully absent from the reform agenda. This absence results from Western experts viewing Congo as they think it should be, based on imported paradigms and world views, instead of accepting it as it is. The expectations of ordinary people are rarely taken into account because they are disassociated from debates about institutional reform. They are political outsiders. This disassociation results from the breach between foreign experts who interact with local elites – the political insiders – and the voiceless hoi polloi. Many expatriate reform actors working towards reform and development have university degrees and experience in economics, management, agronomy and other technical disciplines. Social scientists with cultural sensitivity are under-represented in the corps of reform experts. Jean-Claude Willame emphasized the importance of 'empathy' when trying to comprehend the subtleties of Zairian politics (Willame 1992: 8). His observation remains compelling today.

Congo is a country of contrast and diversity. Roughly half the territory is covered by dense tropical forest, the other by savanna. Ecologically and culturally, the lush green mountains of the east are worlds away from the short Atlantic coast in the west or the southern copper belt area. There are also striking imbalances with respect to population density and demographic distribution. The daily lives of rural people (approximately 50 per cent of the population) are very different from those of the city dwellers of Kinshasa, Lubumbashi or Butembo because of disproportionate access to infrastructure, administration, basic services and entertainment. While the traditional versus modern cleavage is becoming increasingly obscure, it still influences how people live their present and perceive their future. The stratification between political, economic and military elites and ordinary citizens is overwhelming, even though their destinies are intertwined.

There is also a tremendous gap between the super-rich, who are generally urban-based, and the rural poor. Many rural communities live on the fringe or even outside the cash economy. The rural economy itself is extremely varied and comprises artisanal mineral extraction that feeds into international trade networks while in other regions it is based on self-sufficiency and barter. Some Congolese share a common language, others are divided by language. The gender gap is also a social reality. Although women are largely responsible for family survival and cohesion and have become important protagonists in the dominant informal economy, they tend to be sidelined in decision-making processes, whether it is within the family or at the national political level. There were forty-three ministers and vice-ministers in the second Muzito government in 2010: only five were women.

These contrasts contribute to the formation and reproduction of a fragmented social, political and cultural landscape. It is difficult to grasp the subtleties of this landscape and even more difficult to control it. Reform failure is anchored in this fragmented landscape. The analogy of a shattered mirror repieced together captures the image of fragmentation (De Boeck 2004b: 46). Cultural factors determine where individuals fit into the complex web of social networks and hierarchies. They also have direct and indirect impacts on how political systems evolve. Culture is admittedly an intricate, imprecise and ambiguous reality that is not easy to harmonize with concrete reform actions. Nonetheless, foreign experts working in Congo could learn much about the people whose institutions they are trying to reform by integrating culture into their projects and programmes.

Although the cultural environment is always evolving, there are historically embedded and identifiable patterns. These patterns influence contemporary politics. Solidarity networks based on the extended family, clan and tribe are one example. They have developed to facilitate specific ethnic priorities such as job recruitment, political appointments, access to credit, housing for rural migrants and university scholarships. Networks tend to be headed by important traditional figures, chiefs and elders or by well-to-do individuals of an ethnic group. Some of these networks trace their origins to associations going back as far as the early colonial period, formerly called *mutualistes*. The political parties of the late colonial period all had their roots in ethnic associations. These are the factors that led Schatzberg to observe that '[E]thnicity [...] has to be considered in any attempt to treat complex strategies of access and domination' (Schatzberg 1988: 21). Ethnicity in the Congolese context 'needs to be conceptualized as a dynamic framework' and refers to 'a collective recognition of affinity, to which social and emotional meanings are attached' (Young and Turner 1985: 138–9).

One example of this dynamism pertains to the ways in which ethnic-based solidarity is gradually coming under pressure, especially in urban areas. Given the precariousness of life for the vast majority of Congolese, they have been forced to multiply the networks that help them survive. Solidarity is no longer limited solely to members of a family, clan or tribe. It is also extended to inhabitants of a village, an urban neighbourhood, school alumni, members of a religious sect or prayer group or friends in a sports association. While most people are able and willing to extend psychological support, financial and material constraints limit solidarity to a pragmatic system of exchange (Nzeza 2004). People help each other primarily if they can expect something in return. Both old and emerging networks regulate social and political relations because people believe that they have the right to receive and the duty to give (Leclercq 1993: 24–6).

(Dis)information

Information is power. (Dis)information and propaganda are key elements of masquerade and political culture. The way information is controlled, manipulated, retained and broadcast is a close equal to the might of repressive force in Congo. Deciding 'who knows what' and 'who is allowed to know what' is a crucial stake in the political arena. Ensuring that national priorities – such as fundamental debates about politics, accountability and political legitimacy – are not clearly understood by the general public is a specific objective of those in power. Mobutu benefited from the exceptional communication talents of regime spokesman and image-maker Dominique Sakombi to achieve this objective. Sakombi was the archetype of the great communicator in the service of the chief, the bard who flattered and sang praise while skilfully elaborating and disseminating propaganda and misinformation. Lambert Mende, minister of media and communications, is the (dis)information tsar of Joseph Kabila. His role is to give the impression, inside the country and abroad, that all is well in Congo, thanks to the determination and stewardship of President Joseph Kabila.

In 2009 the government banned Radio France International (RFI) from broadcasting in Congo because their programmes allegedly contributed to the demoralization of the national army. RFI did in fact report that former rebel troops who had been integrated into the army deserted over pay grievances. Global Witness, Human Rights Watch and the International Federation of Human Rights responded by criticizing the government's policy of censorship against RFI. Mende retorted in turn by denouncing these NGOs as 'humanitarian terrorists' who repeat lies and whose aim is to 'destabilize' and 'Balkanize' the Congo for financial motives.[1] It was also Mende who refuted the casualty reports put forward by Human Rights Watch after the Enyele rebellions in Equateur province in April 2010. The scenario was repeated again in April 2010 when the Kinshasa authorities downplayed the number of victims of an alleged massacre by the Lord's Resistance Army. Human Rights Watch reported 250 victims. Kinshasa reported twenty-five.[2] In the run-up to the fifty-year independence celebrations and discussions about withdrawing United Nations peacekeepers, it was important for the government's image to mask internal security problems.

The truth or falsehood of official information is only of relative importance. Congolese have learned to be extremely sceptical and suspicious. In some societies, words have more meaning than in others. Achille Mbembe's recommendation to make 'distinctions between what is true and what is false, that which is to be believed and that which is "beyond belief"' (Mbembe 2005/06: 80) is sound advice. People very often say 'I am the brother of Thomas', referring to Jesus's doubting apostle. Rumour may be taken to be the gospel truth and hard facts are sometimes dismissed as prevarications. Congolese have low expectations on being informed of trivial matters and even lower expectations regarding important national issues. Who was behind the assassination of Laurent-Désiré Kabila? Whatever happened to Mobutu's allegedly colossal fortune? Did Joseph Kabila know about plans to eliminate Floribert Chebeya? Will presidential elections really take place in 2011? In many cases people do not believe they will ever know the truth. In others, they prefer not raising questions out of fear: the role of Mobutu's nocturnal assassins, known as *hiboux*, was something that people preferred not to talk about. In some instances, even fairly well-documented events that have shed light on significant national events are relegated to the realm of suspicion and disbelief, such as the circumstances surrounding the murder of Patrice Lumumba (Bustin 2002). Cultivating confusion and misunderstanding, reformulating official explanations with updated ones and sending conflicting messages are clearly identifiable trends in Congolese communication politics.

An uncanny incident in January 2010 left Western diplomats and ordinary Congolese baffled.[3] Canada's ambassador to Kinshasa, Sigrid Anna Johnson, screamed for help from an office inside the presidential palace where she was alone with Adolphe Lumanu, Kabila's cabinet director. Mrs Johnson accused Lumanu of trying to sexually molest her. He retorted that she was trying to seduce him as a means of resolving a high-stake commercial dispute between the Congolese government and First Quantum, a Canadian mining company. The situation is bizarre because if in fact she was willing to go to these extremes for a commercial deal, why would she have screamed? Ottawa sent a high-ranking official to Kinshasa to calm this awkward diplomatic situation. Lumanu was promoted to the important position of minister of the interior shortly after the incident. No public statements were ever made to clarify what really transpired.

The vulnerability of the Kabila regime can be gauged by its absence of transparency. Potential threats emanate from the outside (Rwanda, Angola or the Lord's Resistance Army), from within (rebel militia and opposition movements) and from below (the justifiably disgruntled masses). In this context of vulnerability, those in command are obsessed with controlling the flow of information and clouding facts. They attempt to keep people un- and under-informed. This obsession exists at the summit of the state but it also extends to other levels of society and all walks of life. Congolese, like many other Africans, are reluctant to disclose their intentions – to marry, buy a plot of land, apply for a job or take a trip – out of fear that the forces of the occult will interfere before they can be accomplished. Secrecy is thus a powerful cultural reality and political strategy. 'All over Africa', and Congo is no exception, 'the belief that really effective power is exercised in secret is particularly strong' (Ellis and Ter Haar 2004: 84). The target of international condemnation, Leopold II, ostensibly subscribed to this belief. Before turning the Congo Free State over to Belgium, he ordered the burning of his Congo archives. 'Seldom has a totalitarian regime gone to such lengths to destroy so thoroughly the records of its work' (Hochschild 1998: 294).

Secrecy may make sense for national security reasons but in Congo it is taken to extremes. A major event with repercussions

113

on national security shrouded in secrecy was the deal made between Kabila and President Kagame of Rwanda. It allowed for the incursion of some four thousand Rwandan troops into Congo in 2009 and resulted in extensive violence against civilians, including widespread killings and rapes. Perceived as facilitating the connivances of a fifth column, it reignited questions of Kabila's origins. Is he really Congolese or is he Rwandan? Many critics argue that Kabila is a puppet manipulated by Kagame. This plan sought to address the crisis conditions in the Kivus by integrating the Rwanda-backed Congolese rebel group National Congress for the Defence of the People (CNDP) into the Congolese National Army (FARDC). It also envisaged carrying out a series of ultimately unsuccessful military operations against other militias. The incursion was attacked in parliament and resulted in the removal of its president, Vital Kamerhe. The secret deal, which was designed and implemented under the aegis of Kabila's Katangese advisers, in close partnership with Kigali, can be summarized as: (i) discussions take place between Kabila and Kagame; (ii) Augustin Katumba shuttles back and forth between Kinshasa and Kigali; (iii) John Numbi and his Rwandan counterpart iron out the final details. No attempts were made to engage local communities in a transparent dialogue that could have been an alternative to force.

Secrecy is also a useful political strategy for commercial deal-making. Laurent-Désiré Kabila established a pattern of secrecy with respect to granting mining concessions to support his war effort. His deal-making was contingent upon secrecy as he sometimes awarded the same concession to multiple partners, as revealed by the Lutundula Commission (République démocratique du Congo/Assemblée Nationale 2005: 97).[4] American, Canadian, South African and Zimbabwean companies were the main protagonists during Kabila's war of liberation and in the period that followed his capture of power. Concessions awarded by both Kabila father and son were highly criticized because of the non-transparent terms of agreement, due diligence failure on the part of investors and the unequal nature of benefits that accrued to the mining companies and Congolese political elites with little advantage for the Congolese people. It was for these reasons that the World Bank, human rights NGOs and other international partners insisted that the government carry out a review of the mining concession award process as a follow-up to the Lutundula Commission. The review process was in turn criticized as being non-transparent and manipulated by high-ranking political elites so they could continue their deal-making in the mining sector with minimal oversight. The famous 'deal of the century' made with China was also particularly non-transparent, especially during the negotiation process, even though it was one of Congo's major commercial and development agreements.

Political repression

While the administration had a firm grip on people and territory at the end of the colonial period, the state steadily lost control after independence. Mobutu survived by combining support from external backers with reliance on a network of collaborators who dominated the security and economic sectors. He carved out an image for himself as a deified father figure, *le père de la Nation*, while manipulating the spiritual dimension of power to dominate the political landscape. Mobutu's power was built on fear and gift-giving. His age, flamboyancy, longevity as president and brilliant oratory skills corresponded with Congolese views of political legitimacy. Joseph Kabila has none of these assets. Hampered by a vocal opposition in parliament, he is more discreet, less of a risk taker and apparently uninspired by political ideology. His power, however, like that of Mobutu, is also based on fear and gift-giving.

Just as Mobutu relied on key allies from his own region and ethnic group, Laurent-Désiré Kabila relied on a cadre of Katangese political cronies. Many of Joseph Kabila's key advisers, supporters and party apparatchiks also hail from Katanga. The ruling coalition around President Kabila exploits classic strong-arm methods to maintain power. A small group of political insiders share power, based on reciprocal exploitation and benefits. As elsewhere in Africa and beyond, politics are based on people oppressing others and on the humiliation of exclusion. A heart-rending assessment of Mobutu's despotism retains its pertinence for most Congolese today: 'life is the art of avoiding the worst, in hope of a better day' (Jewsiewicki 1991: 69). Political repression is one of the basic tricks of the trade. There is a deeply rooted political culture of violence in Congo. This manifests itself as rape and mayhem as political strategy in the Kivus, assassination of human rights activists and journalists and deployment of a corps of vicious security and intelligence forces. The Congolese organization Journaliste en danger serves as a constant reminder of limitations on freedom of speech and violence against journalists.[5] Reporters exposing high-level corruption are at particular risk. The president's Republican Guard (Garde républicaine), the National Intelligence Agency (Agence nationale de renseignement – ANR), the Rapid Intervention Police Force (Police d'intervention rapide – PIR) and the Migration Office (Direction générale des migrations – DGM), which controls who goes where in and outside the country, all terrorize the Congolese people. As these services depend directly on the presidency they are not subject to parliamentary oversight or Ministry of Justice scrutiny.

The ANR is a particularly notorious outfit. According to Amnesty International, its agents are among the most frequent torturers in DRC.[6] The ANR's mandate is supposed to be limited to investigating crimes against state security, such as treason, espionage, political crimes or conspiracies. Nonetheless, it regularly harasses people suspected of minor offences to extort money from them. Opposition and civil society activists accused of violating state security are particularly targeted. When activists are arrested, they are held incommunicado in cruel and inhumane conditions with no food or water at secret detention centres. They have no access to legal assistance. Human rights monitors have problems investigating these arrests.

The Republican Guard is another security arm that serves the direct interests of the president and his clan. Usually immune to the brutality of the security forces, people in Kinshasa were shocked by an event that transpired at a busy downtown intersection. Zoe Kabila, the president's brother, ordered his Republican Guard escort to beat up two traffic officers because they did not give his vehicle priority.[7] Terrible indeed, the incident is minor compared to other actions of the Republican Guard. It calls attention to the banality of arbitrary violence in Congo.

Corruption

Corruption clichés from Mobutu's Zaire still have currency. 'The best way to make money is to become a politician.' 'Dishonesty is the prerogative of elites.' 'Those at the top are greedy and corrupt because they never know how long they will be in positions to steal our money.' It has become prosaic to associate corruption with Congo/Zaire, in part because there is some recurrent truth in these clichés. The objective here is not to pursue the ongoing invective against the Congolese political establishment for being corrupt and predatory but to present analysis on how deeply ingrained corruption impedes the implementation of reform initiatives and development. This section also aims to show how corruption and political culture are overlapping realities. The focus here is on Congo but similar arguments and examples could well emerge from other countries. A peripheral but interesting question pertains to why massive corruption has not significantly hampered development and investment in countries like China and Russia, while in Congo it has.

Experts, academics, civil society activists and NGOs have been analysing corruption since the start of state collapse in the late 1970s. Erwin Blumenthal, an IMF expert recruited to head the Bank of Zaire in 1978, was one of the first and best-informed observers of how the Mobutu system institutionalized corruption to maintain political domination and ensure personal enrichment. Referring to the heydays of Mobutu's 'kleptocracy', David Gould argued that institutionalized bureaucratic corruption was the primary cause of Zairean underdevelopment (Gould 1980). Transparency International's Corruption Perceptions Index has been a consistent monitor testifying to the tenacity of corruption from Mobutu to Joseph Kabila. As some key protagonists on

Kinshasa's political landscape today are veterans of the Second Republic, this tenacity is not surprising.

The hypocrisy of masquerade permeates anti-corruption discourse and initiatives. Following in the footsteps of Mobutu's famous *le mal zaïrois* speech in which he harangued his countrymen for having the reputation of being corrupt buffoons, Joseph Kabila launched his own version of 'zero tolerance' in 2009. The president publicly declared war on the misappropriation of public funds, fiscal fraud, embezzlement, graft, influence trafficking, impunity for wrongdoing and bribery. In principle, there are legal provisions to fight and punish corruption. Congo is a member of the UN Anti-Corruption Convention and passed an anti-corruption law in 2004. Additional legislation includes the 2004 Money Laundering Act under which the country cooperates with African and European crime-fighting organizations. In an attempt to show that the government was serious, a number of high-ranking magistrates were fired in 2009 and 2010. But it would be idealistic to take this at face value. The real reasons related to political cleansing – it was a convenient pretext to eliminate opponents and replace them with members from the presidential fold – and grandstanding for both internal and outside consumption.

Bribery is commonplace in public and private business transactions, despite legislation. As described in previous chapters, legal and institutional provisions have very little impact without firm political will. Bribery is a particularly important form of negotiation in the areas of government procurement, dispute settlement and taxation. Private companies bribe the taxman to pay less tax. Justice is awarded to the highest bidder. Given the nature of aid flows into Congo, contract-awarding practices and public procurement of goods and services are a major source of illegal enrichment for government officials. Companies that pay bribes to the officials who participate in committees and commissions for the award of donor contracts have a greater chance of success. This applies to public works projects and the purchase of material and consultancy services. Bribes can take the form of high-percentage under-the-table transfers. Sometimes they can be small-scale gift-giving (cell phones or laptop computers) or discreet services rendered (such as facilitating a visa request or helping a child attend school abroad). Although calls for tender are supposed to be open and public, private companies accept paying for privileged information to prepare their submissions before the competition. Official and semi-official intermediaries thrive on this dependency. Kinshasa has been undergoing a relative construction boom in the past few years. Popular opinion attributes this boom to these forms of corruption. A recently coined expression to describe corrupt high-ranking public officials is *kuluna en cravate* (white-collar crooks).

Corruption and predation go hand in hand and represent one of the commonalities of Congolese history from Leopold II to Joseph Kabila (Kankwenda 2005). Underpaid primary schoolteachers force their pupils to buy snacks from their wives according to the same logic that Kabila's close advisers levy heavy commissions before signing major commercial deals with foreign partners for mining concessions, oil exploration rights or arms sales. Conscious of predation in the workplace, an international food security NGO required its Congolese consultants to open bank accounts for direct salary transfers. The objective was to thwart attempts by senior staff to demand cash kickbacks. Perhaps laudable, the idea was totally ineffective. Once the monthly five-hundred-dollar salary was paid into his back account, one consultant reported that he had to pay half to his supervisor. Otherwise, his contract would not have been renewed the following month.[8] This is a trivial example, but one that reveals how complicated it is for foreign partners to bring about change.

The threefold political sin of corruption, predation and patrimonialism is laid bare by a disturbing deal recently brokered between Congo and two British companies.[9] In flagrant contravention of Congolese legislation that prohibits mineral and petroleum production in national parks, Joseph Kabila signed a presidential decree in 2010 allowing SOCO International and Dominion Petroleum to explore and drill for oil in the Virunga National Park. Virunga is a World Heritage site in eastern Congo and home to endangered mountain gorillas. If the deal goes through, wildlife will be threatened and decades of costly and committed conservation work will be annihilated. SOCO's environmental impact assessment, required by law, made no reference to the park's status as a protected area. The decision is inconsistent with Congolese commitments to nature conservation and was severely criticized by UNESCO chief Irina Bokova. Environment minister José Endundo cynically downplayed the inconsistency, stating 'we'll do everything possible to preserve the park but the Congolese people also have to benefit from the riches under the soil'. Endundo added that if oil activities were excluded from the park, he might seek compensation from rich nations in return for not drilling – another good example of extraversion. Given the high economic stakes on the one hand and the social and environmental impacts and the blow – once again – to Congo's international credibility on the other, it would not be naive to presume that high-ranking officials received bribes.

Extreme poverty and the relative absence of alternative sources of capital accumulation enable corruption to persist and mutate. These problems were used to explain the astonishing success of the Bindo phenomenon in 1990/91 in Kinshasa. 'Bindomania' was a variation of the Ponzi pyramid investment scheme that created great expectations of quick cash but had a devastating effect on the population (Jewsiewicki 1993). Congo is under-industrialized, the service sector is marginal and commerce is small-scale. The perception of government service being a way to financial gain is consequently held by many educated Congolese today, just as it was when the Nigerian Chinua Achebe wrote his classic political novel *Things Fall Apart* a half-century ago. Recruitment into public administration, government service, political office and the peripheral space that encompasses advisers, assistants and sub-contractors entails varying degrees of social promotion and access to money. As the reform process relies on state actors to implement projects and programmes, reform funding paradoxically contributes to corruption. While poverty and insufficient economic alternatives stimulate corruption, corruption in turn produces poverty. It strangles the flow of resources into the national treasury and scares off private investors.

Stakeholders tend to turn a blind eye to corrupt practices. Donors tolerate corruption because it can be more important to spend funding according to the calendar and budget stipulated in a project's terms of reference than to sanction corrupt officials. Practical considerations are more important than ethical ones. Impunity is also endorsed out of concerns for respect of national sovereignty, pseudo-political correctness and even because of low expectations. Congolese opposition groups similarly tend to be relatively discreet when it comes to overtly denouncing governmental corruption, probably because they are patiently waiting in the sidelines to exploit the system themselves. The political culture of *non-dit* (the unsaid) is far more prevalent in Congo than the practice of naming and shaming common in Western democracies. Although good governance has to be the foundation of institutional reform, there are no realistic strategies to force those at the top to abandon their corrupt practices.

6 | Conclusion

The scorpion and the crocodile

From a state-building perspective, the overall message of this book is hardly optimistic. There are some examples of commitment and good technical and institutional reform initiatives but there are few indicators of successful reform results. There is very little evidence that isolated success stories or the astonishing Congolese potential have produced tangible social dividends or more efficient and accountable institutions. The parable of the crocodile and the scorpion presented at the beginning of the book evokes some of the challenges that continue to undermine the reform and state-building process. It is useful in highlighting many of Congo's old and new sufferings.[1] Foreign partners and African elites can be associated with the scorpion. The unlucky crocodile, the victim, can be interpreted as being the people of Africa. A contrasting interpretation is also possible. The scorpion, Africa, has deceived outside partners, particularly those in the West, into perpetuating an unworkable development model.

The most striking problem today is the powerlessness of stakeholders to influence Congo's unmanageable political landscape. International partners design, fund and carry out programmes whose evaluations reveal a startling degree of inefficiency. The gap between strategies and impacts remains wide. Congo's partners are powerless to induce the real change that is needed to improve the well-being of the population. They have also proved powerless to impose new visions of governance upon a reluctant political establishment. Partners have demonstrated their capacity to promote new discourses about good governance but not to implement the policies themselves. With the exception of a few international companies, the foreign private sector is also powerless to take advantage of Congo's great investment possibilities. The absence of investment-enabling conditions remains a major problem.

The political class itself, despite its efforts to consolidate and reproduce its own supremacy, is also powerless and vulnerable. The quasi-democratic gains achieved through elections accrued to a small faction of political actors at the national and provincial levels. Elected officials share, dispute and manipulate democratic dividends with little consideration for the needs of ordinary people, who are kept outside the political arena. The government has not achieved workable political compromises with the parliamentary opposition; it has been unable to garner the respect and credibility of its international partners; it has been powerless to respond to the expectations of its constituency, particularly in the fundamental areas of security and economic development.

The parable also evokes the tragedy of self-destruction. Post-colonial Congo has experienced many phases of extreme violence that can be equated with social suicide. The bloody rebellions of the mid-1960s, the brutality of the Mobutu dictatorship, the looting sprees that shook Kinshasa in the early 1990s and the two recent wars are the most obvious examples. Social cannibalism is a rampant phenomenon. Society is its own prey, feeding off itself. The way that security forces and civil servants feed off the population for enrichment and survival is further proof.

The crocodile, either through naivety or irrationality, made the ultimate sacrifice of giving up its life. Sacrifice is omnipresent in Congo. The term refers to the hard reality of doing without, absence and emptiness. People do without basic necessities such as food, health, adequate primary education and safe drinking water. They do without real political participation, physical security, leisure or the ability to organize their time as they would like. Parents are not only forced to decide what child will be able to go to school in a given year, sometimes they have to decide who shall eat and who shall go hungry.

Misunderstanding is another element of the predicament. The crocodile misunderstood the scorpion's capacity for self-destruction. Congo's Western backers, particularly in the period when they were heavily involved in legitimizing Joseph Kabila, miscalculated his potential to sidetrack the democratic agenda that he was supposed to implement. Misunderstanding also results from diverging perceptions of the need to change between Western partners and the Congolese authorities. The latter seek to maintain their positions at all costs; the former stubbornly struggle to inculcate the need to change in a political culture and society that they do not understand – in part because of different world views and belief systems. The whole spectrum of partners – NGOs, traditional bilateral actors and multilateral donors – persists in wanting to transform a political establishment that opposes change and in trying to develop a deprived population that has not been consulted.

Fragile agency

Congo is one of the worst humanitarian tragedies of the new millennium. The post-colonial state was designed to be a provider of social services but gradually mutated into a social predator. For the last twenty years of Mobutu's dictatorship, collapse, oppression, corruption and criminalization were terms used to express state failure in sub-Saharan Africa's largest territory. The situation did not improve under Laurent-Désiré Kabila. Expert observers and ordinary Congolese are increasingly drawing parallels between the Zaire of Mobutu and the Third Republic Congo of Joseph Kabila. The main similarity is power first, the common good after. The post-colonial state-building enterprise has not resulted in the establishment of a Weberian political order with a functioning bureaucracy, a balance between executive, judiciary and parliamentary powers and efficient public servants or law enforcement agents.

But this does not mean that Congo is a place of utter chaos and hopelessness. Another interpretation of the social and political environment is indeed possible. Congo is a world of multiple logics where remarkable patterns of stability, organization and quest for well-being are emerging (Trefon 2004). There is order in the disorder. These patterns have arisen in spite of, and owing to, state failure and conflict. State–society relations are evolving at all social and political levels in a context where function and dysfunction intersect and overlap. New forms of social organization are taking shape to compensate for the overwhelming failures of the post-colonial state. Social organization is a rapidly shifting process that enables ordinary Congolese to simply carry on with life and get things done. This dynamic process entails juxtaposing opportunities and interests, capitalizing on old alliances and creating new networks.

The capacity of people to influence their own destinies, to act independently and make choices for themselves and their families – a concept in sociology referred to as agency – is a powerful social reality. Agency in Congo today contrasts sharply with the rigid colonial structures that inculcated a paternalistic work ethic, missionary education and the values of Christianity, and the establishment of racial and class segregation and strict gender roles. Innovative forms of solidarity networks, commercial accommodation and interdependencies became apparent in the early 1990s, particularly in urban Congo. They go well beyond the survival economy that took form in the mid-1980s in response to the then emerging multiform crisis. These promising social phenomena are nonetheless still hampered by tension, suspicion, violence and betrayal. Although social reinvention contributes to very basic survival at the individual and family level, it is not yet contributing to broader sustainable economic and political development of the type elaborated and advocated by Western development theorists.

Momentum for positive change results from people and their social dynamism, not from government or external interventions. The Congo state is indeed failed, but in striking contrast, Congolese society is strong, tolerant, creative, generous and vibrant. Historically and universally, social dynamism germinates from the blending of demographic, economic, religious and cultural factors. In independent Congo, demographic growth and urbanization, the emergence of the informal economy, profound attachments to belief systems and religion and popular culture in the form of music and artistic expression are the vital ingredients of being Congolese.

Grassroots associations, local and international NGOs and community-based solidarity networks have multiplied significantly since the 1990s. They have formed the basis for an emerging civil society. The phenomenon developed because people had no alternative but to invent new social and economic survival strategies. These networks help replace the state in many areas of public life. Agency is reflected in the networks that facilitate access to credit, land, housing, used clothing from international charities, heath and education. Cooperatives improve food security in the areas of production, transportation and marketing. They also play important roles in bridging rural and urban communities. Despite the huge numbers of affiliates, however, DRC's civil society is far from being a genuine one where people are citizens claiming rights instead of clients seeking access to random benefits in an arbitrary negotiation process. Civil society components are fragmented and divided by competing interests. The country is still beleaguered by the corrupted social, political and economic situation.

It seems paradoxical that increased civil society activity has not resulted in positive political change. While civil society is timidly making its voice heard in terms of social and political mobilization, weaknesses persist. Its leaders, who are often intimidated, bullied and manipulated by the ruling political class, tend to lack experience and professionalism. There is an absence of a critical mass of competent actors. Women, who could be drivers of positive change, are marginalized and under-represented in civil society forums. Funding constraints also continue to hamper the growth of civil society. The little funding that is available often comes from foreign sources. This reproduces the problems of aid agendas and dependency. Another form of dependency is the dominance of urban elites who claim to represent rural communities but who in reality are disconnected from their rural bases. Civil society is not immune to the poor coordination between donor and development actors. One of the most serious threats to attaining civil society maturity in Congo today is the absence of collaboration between civil society actors and government. Their relationship is undermined by mistrust and rivalry. This harsh environment necessitates strategic revisions and significant capacity-building if civil society actors are to play a more determinant role in politics, peace-building, poverty alleviation and gender equality.

State crisis, insecurity and lack of economic opportunities force Congolese to seek their fortunes abroad. The hope that the vast majority have of a better life outside Congo is an impressive commentary on perceptions of the future and the incapacity of the state to respect its development mission. Families invest in strategies that allow for at least one member to migrate. The dominant push to migrate is clearly economic but the prestige – be it real or imagined – of having a relative in Europe is also a motivation. In Lingala (the main language spoken in Kinshasa) *lola* translates as both 'paradise' and 'Europe'. Belgium, France, the USA, Canada and South Africa have been the primary destinations over the past twenty years. Congolese diaspora populations are active in politics – usually opposition politics – as is witnessed by their organization of anti-Kabila demonstrations and animated debates on Internet forums. The Internet and mobile phones facilitate communication between migrants and family back home, which fosters and perpetuates family bonds and political networking. But unlike in many other African countries where diaspora remittances are used for development, in Congo they serve to help families cope with everyday poverty (De Bruyn et al. 2008; Sumata et al. 2004).

Religion is a major source of social solidarity, political awareness-raising and well-being. It has figured prominently in Congo's politics since colonial times. About 80 per cent of Congolese are Christian, predominantly Roman Catholic and Protestant. The magnitude of the Catholic Church's economic and social role is demonstrated by the fact that even after the collapse of state structures and institutions, it was a significant provider of healthcare

Conclusion

and education. It has played a particularly important political role too. The Catholic Church organized peaceful anti-Mobutu demonstrations in Kinshasa that aroused popular sentiment and mobilization in the 1990s. In 2010 Laurent Monsengwo was elevated to the rank of cardinal. His publicly declared opposition to proposed revisions of the constitution and his denunciation of the general political climate just after his consecration have been an embarrassment to President Kabila.[2]

Most non-Christians follow either traditional religions or syncretic sects. Witchcraft and sorcery remain essential social realities. Syncretic sects combine Christianity with traditional beliefs and rituals. The most popular of these sects is Kimbanguism with its 3 million followers. Since the early 1990s, numerous prayer groups, exorcists, messianic and prophetic churches and evangelists have proliferated, especially in urban areas. These movements are popular not just among the poor. They also recruit among members of the political and security establishment. The spiritual leaders of these Christian 'neo-communities' are opinion makers who occupy increasingly important positions of power. As poverty and crisis are propitious for the manipulation of belief systems, they cater to the need of many Congolese to seek redemption, salvation and atonement. Joseph Kabila's appointment of Methodist pastor Ngoy Mulunda, one of his very close advisers, head of the National Independent Electoral Commission is an indication of the overlap between the spiritual and the political spheres.

The constitution guarantees freedom of speech and expression but greater access to political information and debate has its limits. A certain tolerance of social and political grumbling is possible as long as it does not impinge upon the prerogatives of political power. International human rights organizations have been helpful in fostering freedom of expression, in part by training journalists. As a result, media have been able to criticize the government, highlight social problems and inform people about political events and actors. Several daily newspapers are published in Kinshasa and there are more than one hundred private radio stations, some of which broadcast news. Cheap Chinese transistor radios are easily available and provide the dominant source of information throughout the country.

Civil society activists are increasingly using the Internet to organize exchanges and ideas about politics and development.[3] Anyone with a computer or a cell phone has some degree of power. Congolese at home and abroad are integrated into the age of new technologies. Social media, blogging and microblogging could have positive and far-reaching implications for political awakening as they have elsewhere in Africa and the Middle East. People are relearning, reinterpreting and spreading the message that oppression is not sustainable. Just days following the amendment of the constitution in January 2011, Congolese opposition groups demonstrated in London, Paris and Brussels. These new media technologies facilitated the organization of these demonstrations. These communication platforms are something to track as access to them becomes more widespread. People have taken to the streets on numerous occasions already in Kinshasa, mainly driven by frenzy and anger (de Villers and Omasombo 2004; Devisch 1995). It is not unlikely that they will do so again, transforming anger into the will for positive change. In the future, taking to the streets could be inspired by organized leadership with clearly defined political objectives.

Congo is on the move. While we may not know where it is going, few observers would deny that state–society relations are evolving rapidly. The institutional future of the country is uncertain and there are no convincing prospects for a New Deal. Congo could be heading towards another dictatorship and new forms of oppression. Nonetheless, people appear to be seizing opportunities to improve their destinies by redefining the dynamics of their social interactions. Whatever type of new state system emerges over time, it will have to accommodate the specificities of Congolese history and culture with universal models of democracy. This would entail giving voice both to the individual, which is the cornerstone of Western liberal democracies, and the group, which is a major constitutive factor in Congolese and African political, economic and social life. Although the social cost of crisis in the Congo is overwhelming, it has helped people appropriate the sentiment of being Congolese. There is a Congolese nation, fragmented and plural indeed, yet with an emerging sense of collective belonging and future. It will take a very long time to heal the trauma and humiliation of poverty, war and political exclusion, but perhaps the sentiment of being Congolese can be transformed into the positive energy needed to reinvent the state and strengthen society.

Notes

1 Why state-building is not working in the Congo

1 news.bbc.co.uk/2/hi/8347503.stm, accessed 15 May 2010.

2 www.freedomhouse.org/template.cfm?page=22&year=2010&country=7954, accessed 5 December 2010.

3 www.congoforum.be/fr/nieuwsdetail.asp?subitem=1&newsid=171563&Actualiteit=selected, accessed 10 February 2011.

2 The political economy of broken promises

1 Welcoming remarks at the UN Security Council Session on the DRC, New York, 24 January 2000.

2 This observation was confirmed by the Congolese newspaper *Le Phare* on 21 September 2010.

3 www.rtbf.be/info/media/wikileaks/wikileaks-j-kabila-avait-une-aversion-envers-k-de-gucht-302654, accessed 8 February 2011.

4 www.syfia-grands-lacs.info/index.php5?view=articles&action=voir&idArticle=1776, accessed 1 December 2010.

5 www.congoforum.be/fr/nieuwsdetail.asp?subitem=1&newsid=169042&Actualiteit=selected, accessed 9 July 2010.

6 www.globalwitness.org/campaigns/conflict/conflict-minerals/democratic-republic-congo, accessed 3 February 2011.

7 www.mineweb.com/mineweb/view/mineweb/en/page 36?oid=99695&sn=Detail, accessed 4 February 2011.

8 web.worldbank.org/external/projects/main?Projectid=P106982&theSitePK=349466&piPK=6429041 5&pagePK=64283627&menuPK=642 82134&Type=Overview, accessed 4 February 2011.

9 www.sec.gov/about/laws/wall streetreform-cpa.pdf, accessed 4 February 2011.

10 FLEGT is a voluntary scheme to ensure that only legally harvested timber is imported into the EU. See ec.europa.eu/environ-ment/forests/flegt.htm, accessed 4 February 2011.

11 Information on the Independent Observatory is available at: www.rdc-conversiontitres forestiers.org/en/docman/rapports /23.html, accessed 4 February 2011.

12 eiti.org/, accessed 4 February 2011.

13 www.doingbusiness.org/data/exploreeconomies/congo,-dem~-rep~, accessed 10 January 2011.

14 www.heritage.org/index/ Ranking, accessed 10 January 2011.

3 A patchwork of unrealistic reforms

1 The term 'excess deaths' refers to the number of people dying in excess of the average mortality rate in a given region for similar income levels.

2 CIAT was an executive body mandated to accompany the transitional government in elaborating political, economic and security strategies. It played a key role in organizing the electoral process. Its mandate expired at the official end of the transition period.

3 Much of the information on dates and actions during these phases comes from Clément (2009a) and Hoebeke et al. (2009).

4 Information available at: static.rnw.nl/migratie/www. rnw.nl/internationaljustice/ icc/DRC/080429-ICC-Ntaganda-redirected, accessed 5 May 2010.

5 According to BBC news. news.bbc.co.uk/2/hi/africa/8650112. stm, accessed 8 May 2010.

6 www.solutions-site.org/ artman/publish/article_495.shtml, accessed 15 May 2010.

7 Opposition politicians were quick to recall that Article 220 of the constitution strictly forbids any amendments that reduce the prerogatives of the provinces. Nonetheless, the constitution was amended in January 2011, 'legalizing' this reduction.

8 CongoForum, www.congo forum.be/fr/nieuwsdetail.asp?sub item=1&newsid=167007&Actualiteit =selected, accessed 22 April 2010.

9 This imbalance continues to keep secessionist tendencies alive. In July 2010, more than twenty people were arrested in the Katangese capital Lubumbashi because they were demonstrating in favour on an independent Katanga; radiook api.net/ actualite/2010/07/11/lubumbashi-arrestation-d%E2%80%99une-vingtaine-de-personnes-reclamant-l%E2%80%99independance-du-katanga/, accessed 12 July 2010.

10 Law no. 011/2002 of 29 August 2002 is commonly referred to as the Forestry Code.

11 A few of the big companies, some of which have multiple concessions, are Parqueafrique (Italian), ITB (Lebanese), Safbois (American), SIFORCO (German), SODEFOR (Portuguese) and SOFORMA (Swiss).

12 The major NGOs in this context are Greenpeace and the London-based Rainforest Foundation.

13 Information about the observatory is available at www. rdc-conversiontitresforestiers.org, accessed 15 October 2010.

14 www.congoforum.be/fr/ nieuwsdetail.asp?subitem=1&new sid=169566&Actualiteit=selected, accessed 1 October 2010.

4 The administrative juggernaut

1 In addition to library research, this chapter is based on

extensive interviews conducted in rural and urban Congo since 2006.

2 Personal communication, Stylianos Moshinas, PhD student, Bristol University.

3 The United Nations Development Programme put forward the number of 115,599; www.cd.undp.org/projet.aspx?titre=Recensement%20biom%C3%A9trique&projetid=34, accessed 5 October 2010.

4 There a few exceptions. See, for example, Denis Tull (2005) on the reconfiguration of political order in North Kivu, a World Bank report (2005) on good governance and public service, Chapter 4 in Rubbers (2009), which provides analysis of the relations between expatriate business people and the Katangese tax authorities, and an anthropology of the population service of the Lubumbashi town hall (Bussers 2001).

5 Culture matters

1 See the letter sent by Human Rights Watch's Anneke van Woudenberg addressed to Prime Minister Adolpe Muzito, 31 July 2009, www.hrw.org/en/news/2009/07/31/letter-prime-minister-dr-congo-regarding-public-attacks-human-rights-organizations, accessed 13 December 2010.

2 iwpr.net/report-news/kinshasa-downplaying-alleged-massacre, accessed 15 December 2010.

3 afrique.kongotimes.info/rdc/adolphe-lumanu-a-tente-de-violer-sigrid-anna-johnson.html, accessed 15 December 2010.

4 The report of the Lutundula Commission is available at www.freewebs.com/congo-kinshasa/, accessed 17 December 2010.

5 www.jed-afrique.org/fr/#, accessed 8 December 2010.

6 allafrica.com/stories/2009070 21121.html, accessed 8 December 2010.

7 La Voix des sans Voix, press release, 20 October 2010.

8 Interview, Kinshasa, November 2010.

9 www.reuters.com/article/idUSTRE6AP3KA20101126, accessed 28 December 2010.

6 Conclusion

1 Heard in other African contexts with different animals, this version has been analysed elsewhere. See Ilunga Kabongo (1984).

2 www.cardinalrating.com/cardinal_251.htm, accessed 20 January 2011.

3 DRC's civil society portal (www. societecivile.cd) is one example.

Bibliography

Achebe, C. (1959) *Things Fall Apart*, London: Heinemann.

Aloko Gbody Ombeng (1987/88) 'Les petits fonctionnaires zaïrois et le statut du personnel de carrière des services publics de l'Etat: problématique de la mise en œuvre d'un modèle de fonction publique au niveau subalterne', Unpublished PhD thesis, University of Brussels.

Anderson, L. (2005) 'International engagement in failed states: choices and trade-offs', Copenhagen: Danish Institute for International Studies.

Andrews, C., B. Bocoum and D. Tshimena (2008) 'Democratic Republic of Congo: growth with governance in the mining sector', World Bank report no. 43402-ZR.

Autessere, S. (2010) *The Trouble with the Congo: Local Violence and the Failure of International Peacebuilding*, New York: Cambridge University Press.

Bayart, J.-F. (1993) *The State in Africa: The Politics of the Belly*, London: Longman.

— (2000) 'Africa in the world: a history of extraversion', *African Affairs*, 99(395): 217–67.

Bierschenk, T. and J.-P. Olivier de Sardan (1997) 'Local powers and a distant state in rural Central African Republic', *Journal of Modern African Studies*, 35(3): 441–68.

Blundo, G. (2002) 'Editorial. La gouvernance au quotidien en Afrique: les services publics et collectifs et leurs usagers', *Le Bulletin de l'APAD*, 23/24: 1–13.

Blundo, G. and J.-P. Olivier de Sardan (2001) 'La corruption au quotidien en Afrique de l'Ouest', *Politique africaine*, 83: 8–37.

Bongeli Yeikelo Ya Ato, E. (2008) *D'un Etat-bébé à un Etat congolais responsable*, Paris: L'Harmattan.

Bouvier, P. with F. Bomboko (2004) *Le Dialogue intercongolais. Anatomie d'une négociation à la lisière du chaos. Contributions à la théorie de la négociation*, Tervuren/Paris: Institut africain-CEDAF/L'Harmattan.

Bratton, M. and N. van de Walle (1997) *Democratic Experiments in Africa*, Cambridge: Cambridge University Press.

Brautigan, D. (2009) *The Dragon's Gift: The Real Story of China in Africa*, Oxford/New York: Oxford University Press.

Bruneau, J.-C. and T. Simon

(1991) 'Zaïre, l'espace écartelé', *Mappemonde*, 4: 1–5.

Bussers, M. (2001) 'Etat des lieux administratif de la ville de Lubumbashi: enjeux et défaillances des services de l'état civil dans une perspective de transition démocratique', Unpublished Master's thesis, University of Liège.

Bustin, E. (2002) 'Remembrance of sins past: unraveling the murder of Patrice Lumumba', *Review of African Political Economy*, 29(93/94): 537–60.

Calderisi, R. (2006) *The Trouble with Africa: Why Foreign Aid isn't Working*, New Haven, CT: Yale University Press.

Chabal, P. and J.-P. Daloz (1999) *Africa Works: Disorder as Political Instrument*, Oxford: James Currey.

— (2006) *Culture Troubles: Politics and the Interpretation of Meaning*, London: Hurst.

Clapham, C., G. Mills and J. Herbst (2006) *Big African States: Angola, DRC, Ethiopia, Nigeria, South Africa, Sudan*, Johannesburg: University of Witwatersrand Press.

Clément, C. (2009a) 'The EU mission to provide advice and assistance to security sector reform in the Democratic Republic of Congo (EUSEC RD Congo)', in G. Grevi, D. Helly and D. Keohane (eds), *European Security and Defence Policy: The First Ten Years (1999–2009)*, Paris: Institute for Security Studies.

— (2009b) 'Security sector reform in the DRC: forward to the past', in H. Born and A. Schnabel, *Security Sector Reform in Challenging Environments*, Geneva: Geneva Centre for the Democratic Control of Armed Forces.

Clément, J. A. P. (2004) 'The Democratic Republic of the Congo: lessons and challenges for a country emerging from war', in J. A. P. Clément, *Postconflict Economics in sub-Saharan Africa: Lessons from the Democratic Republic of the Congo*, Washington, DC: International Monetary Fund.

Cros, M.-F. (2010a) 'Albert II ira à Kinshasa en juin', *La Libre Belgique*, 11 March.

— (2010b) 'Décentralisation au Congo: l'échec?', *La Libre Belgique*, 14 April.

Dabo, S. (2010) 'L'insatiable Kabila', *Le Pays*, 27 April.

Darbon, D. (2002) 'La culture administrative en Afrique: la construction historique des significations du "phénomène bureaucratique"', *Cadernos de Estudos Africanos*, 3: 65–92.

— (2003) 'Réformer ou reformer les administrations projetées des Afriques? Entre routine anti-politique et ingénierie politique contextuelle', *Revue française d'administration publique*, 105/106: 135–52.

De Boeck, F. (2004a) 'On being *shege* in Kinshasa: children, the occult and the street in Kinshasa', in T. Trefon (ed.),

Reinventing Order in the Congo: How People Respond to State Failure in Kinshasa, London: Zed Books.

— (2004b) *Kinshasa: Tales of the Invisible City*, Ghent: Ludion.

De Bruyn, T., J. Wets, H. Plessers and D. Sorrosa (2008) 'Diaspora involvement in development cooperation. The case of Belgium and the Democratic Republic of Congo (DRC)', Geneva: International Organization for Migration.

Delcourt, L. (2008) 'Aide au développement de l'Union européenne: perspective critique', in L. Delcourt (ed.), *L'Aide européenne. Points de vue critiques du Sud sur la coopération au développement de l'Union Européenne dans ses discours et ses actes*, Louvain-la-Neuve: Centre Tricontinental/Editions Syllepse.

Delta I Consulting (2002) 'Etude sur la réforme de la fonction publique de la République démocratique du Congo', Unpublished report.

de Saint Moulin, L. (1988) 'Histoire de l'organisation administrative du Zaïre', *Zaïre-Afrique*, 28(224): 197–222.

Devers, D. and J.-P. Vande weghe (eds) (2006) *Les Forêts du Bassin du Congo: Etat des Forêts 2006*, Partenariat des Forêts pour le Bassin du Congo, Kinshasa: COMIFAC/European Commission/USAID/Coopération Française.

de Villers, G. (2009) *République démocratique du Congo. De la guerre aux élections: l'ascension de Joseph Kabila et la Troisième République (janvier 2001–août 2008)*, Tervuren/Paris: Institut africain-CEDAF/L'Harmattan.

de Villers, G. and J. Omasombo (2004) 'When Kinois take to the streets', in T. Trefon (ed.), *Reinventing Order in the Congo: How People Respond to State Failure in Kinshasa*, London: Zed Books.

Devisch, R. (1995) 'Frenzy, violence and ethical renewal in Kinshasa', *Public Culture*, 7(3): 593–629.

DfID and Environment and Development Group (2008) 'Directives pour l'évaluation de l'impact environnemental et social des projets routiers en RDC', Unpublished report.

Dibwe dia Mwemba, D. (2002) 'Processus d'informalisation. Le cas de Lubumbashi', in G. de Villers, B. Jewsiewicki and L. Monnier (eds), *Manières de Vivre: Economie de la 'débrouille' dans les villes du Congo/Zaïre*, Tervuren/Paris: MRAC/L'Harmattan.

— (2006) 'La collecte des sources orales: expérience d'enquêtes relatives au conflits Katangais–Kasaïens du Katanga (1991–1994)', *Civilisations*, 54(1/2): 45–55.

Diouf, M. (2002) 'Les poissons ne peuvent pas voter un budget pour l'achat des hameçons. Espace public, corruption et constitution de l'Afrique comme objet scientifique', *Le Bulletin de l'APAD*, 23/24: 23–41.

Dunn, K. (2003) *Imagining the Congo: The International Relations of Identity*, New York: Palgrave Macmillan.

Easterly, D. (2006) *The White Man's Burden: Why the West's efforts to aid the rest have done so much ill and so little good*, New York: Penguin Books.

Eizenstat, S. E., J. E. Porter and J. M. Weinstein (2005) 'Rebuilding weak states', *Foreign Affairs*, 84(1): 134–46.

Ellis, S. and G. Ter Haar (2004) *Worlds of Power: Religious Thought and Political Practice in Africa*, Johannesburg: Wits University Press.

Englebert, P. (2003) 'Why Congo persists: sovereignty, globalization and the violent reproduction of a weak state', Queen Elizabeth House working paper series no. 95.

— (2009) *Africa: Unity, Sovereignty and Sorrow*, Boulder, CO/London: Lynne Rienner.

Englebert, P. and D. M. Tull (2008) 'Postconflict reconstruction in Africa: flawed ideas about failed states', *International Security*, 32(4): 106–39.

Fearon, J. D. and D. D. Laitin (2004) 'Neotrusteeship and the problem of weak states', *International Security*, 28(4): 5–43.

French, H. (2010) 'The next empire', *The Atlantic*, May.

Frère, M.-S. (2009a) 'Appui au secteur des médias: quel bilan pour quel avenir?', in T.

Trefon (ed.), *Réforme au Congo (RDC): Attentes et désillusions*, Tervuren/Paris: Musée royal de l'Afrique centrale/L'Harmattan.

— (2009b) *Elections et Médias en Afrique centrale: Voie des urnes, voix de la paix?*, Paris: Karthala/Institut Panos Paris.

Gettleman, J. (2010) 'Frenzy of rape in Congo reveals UN weakness', *New York Times*, 3 October.

Ghani, A. and C. Lockhart (2008) *Fixing Failed States: A Framework for Rebuilding a Fractured World*, New York: Oxford University Press.

Gillies, A. and R. Joseph (2009) 'Smart Aid: the search for transformation strategies', in R. Joseph and A. Gillies (eds), *Smart Aid for African Development*, Boulder, CO: Lynne Rienner.

Glennie, J. (2008) *The Trouble with Aid: Why Less Could Mean More for Africa*, London: Zed Books.

Global Witness (2009) 'Forest concession cancellations in DR Congo: welcome, but widespread reforms still needed', Unpublished report.

Gons, J. (2004) 'Structural and sectoral policies and their sequencing', in J. A. P. Clément (ed.), *Postconflict Economics in sub-Saharan Africa: Lessons from the Democratic Republic of the Congo*, Washington, DC: International Monetary Fund.

Gould, D. J. (1980) *Bureaucratic Corruption and Underdevelopment in the Third World: The*

Case of Zaire, New York: Pergamon Press.

Herbst, J. (2000) *States and Power in Africa: Comparative Lessons in Authority and Control*, Princeton, NJ: Princeton University Press.

Herbst, J. and G. Mills (2009a) 'There is no Congo: why the only way to help Congo is to stop pretending it exists', *Foreign Policy*, March.

— (2009b) 'Time to end the Congo charade', *Foreign Policy*, August.

Hilary, J. (2008) 'Building a failed state?', *Guardian*, 14 February.

Hills, A. (2009) *Policing Post-Conflict Cities*, London: Zed Books.

Hochschild, A. (1998) *King Leopold's Ghost: A Story of Greed, Terror and Heroism in Colonial Africa*, Boston, MA, and New York: Houghton Mifflin.

Hoebeke, H., H. Boshoff and K. Vlassenroot (2009) '"Monsieur le Président, vous n'avez pas d'armée ...": évaluation de la réforme du secteur de sécurité et de son impact dans les provinces du Kivu', in T. Trefon (ed.), *Réforme au Congo (RDC): Attentes et désillusions*, Tervuren/Paris: Musée royal de l'Afrique centrale/L'Harmattan.

Hugeux, V. (2010) 'RDC. Qui détient la réalité du pouvoir dans ce pays: le système Kabila', *Dialogue*, 12 December.

Human Rights Watch (2008) 'We will crush you: the restriction of political space in the Democratic Republic of Congo', New York: Human Rights Watch.

Ilunga Kabongo (1984) 'Déroutante Afrique ou la syncope d'un discours', *Canadian Journal of African Studies*, 18(1): 13–22.

International Bank for Reconstruction and Development/ World Bank (2010) 'The Democratic Republic of Congo's infrastructure: a continental perspective', Washington, DC: International Bank for Reconstruction and Development/ World Bank.

International Crisis Group (2006) 'Escaping the conflict trap: promoting good governance in the Congo', Africa report no. 114, Nairobi/Brussels.

— (2007) 'Congo: consolidating the peace', Africa report no. 128, Nairobi/Brussels.

— (2010) 'Congo: l'enlisement du projet démocratique', Policy briefing no. 73, Nairobi/Brussels.

International Rescue Committee (2008) 'Mortality in the Democratic Republic of Congo: an ongoing crisis', New York: International Rescue Committee.

Iyaka Buntine, F.-X. (2010) 'Les politiques des réformes administratives en République démocratique du Congo (1990–2010)', Unpublished PhD thesis, Catholic University of Leuven.

Jewsiewicki, B. (1991) 'La mémoire', in C. Coulon and

D.-C. Martin, *Les Afriques Politiques*, Paris: La Découverte.

— (1993) 'Jeux d'argent et de pouvoir au Zaïre: la "bindomanie" et le crépuscule de la Deuxième République', *Politique africaine*, 46: 55–70.

Joseph, R. and A. Gillies (eds) (2009) *Smart Aid for African Development*, Boulder, CO: Lynne Rienner.

Kahola, O. (2006) 'Une semaine d'enquêtes ethnographiques dans les commissariats de Lubumbashi', *Civilisations*, 54(1/2): 25–32.

Kankwenda, M. J. (2005) *L'Economie politique de la prédation au Congo-Kinshasa: des origines à nos jours, 1885–2003*, Kinshasa: ICREDES.

Kavanagh, M. J. (2010) 'World Bank's IFC halts Congo investments until dispute resolved', *Bloomberg Businessweek*, 23 February.

Kobia, R. (2002) 'European Union Commission policy in the DRC', *Review of African Political Economy*, 29(93/94): 431–43.

Kragelund, P. (2009) 'Knocking on a wide-open door: Chinese investments in Africa', *Review of African Political Economy*, 36(122): 479–97.

La Dernière Heure (2010) 9 July.

La Libre Belgique (2010) 27 January.

Lambert, A. and L. Lohlé-Tart (2008) 'La surmortalité au Congo (RDC) durant les troubles de 1998–2004: une estimation des décès en surnombre, scientifiquement fondée à partir des méthodes de la démographie', Unpublished report.

Lancaster, C. (2009) 'How smart are aid donors? The case of the United States', in R. Joseph and A. Gillies (eds), *Smart Aid for African Development*, Boulder, CO: Lynne Rienner.

Laporte, C. (2010) *La Libre Belgique*, 30 June.

Leclercq, H. (1993) 'L'économie populaire informelle de Kinshasa: approche macroéconomique', *Zaïre-Afrique*, 271: 17–36.

Lefever, E. W. (1967) *Uncertain Mandate: Politics of the UN Congo Operation*, Baltimore, MD: Johns Hopkins University Press.

Lemarchand, R. (2009) *The Dynamics of Violence in Central Africa*, Philadelphia: University of Pennsylvania Press.

Le Phare (2010) 21 September.

Le Potentiel (2010) 31 May.

Le Soir (2009) 22 May.

Loore, F. (2007) 'Un long fleuve pas si tranquille', *&CO le magazine de la Coopération belge en République démocratique du Congo*, 3.

Malele Mbala, S. and A. Karsenty (2009) 'Forest revenue decentralisation and the redistribution of profits in the Democratic Republic of Congo', in L. A. German, A. Karsenty and A.-M. Tiani (eds), *Governing Africa's Forests in a Globalized World*, London: Earthscan.

Bibliography

Bibliography

Marchal, J.-N., J. Barut and R. Bimwala (2007) 'Mission d'évaluation du projet. Appui au programme national d'urgence de renforcement des capacités', Unpublished report, PNUD-RDC/Département des Nations unies pour le développement économique et social.

Marriage, Z. (2006) *Not Breaking the Rules, Not Playing the Game: International Assistance to Countries at War*, London: Hurst.

Marysse, S. (2005) 'Decentralization issues in post-conflict Democratic Republic of the Congo (DRC)', in F. Reyntjens and S. Marysse (eds), *L'Afrique des Grands Lacs, Annuaire 2004–2005*, Paris: L'Harmattan.

Marysse, S. and S. Geenen (2009) 'Win-win or unequal exchange? The case of the Sino-Congolese cooperation agreements', *Journal of Modern African Studies*, 47(3): 371–96.

Marysse, S., K. Verbeke, T. de Herdt, O. Tshiunza Mbiye, M. Visser and W. Mariot (2010) 'Evaluation de l'allégement de la dette en RDC', Unpublished report, Antwerp.

Mazalto, M. (2009) 'De la réforme du secteur minier à celle de l'Etat', in T. Trefon (ed.), *Réforme au Congo (RDC): Attentes et Désillusions*, Tervuren/Paris: Musée royal de l'Afrique centrale/L'Harmattan.

Mbaya Mudimba and F. Streiffeler (1999) *Secteur Informel au Congo-Kinshasa: Stratégies pour un développement endogène*, Kinshasa: Editions universitaires africaines.

Mbembe, A. (2005/06) 'Variations on the beautiful in the Congolese world of sounds', *Politique africaine*, 100: 71–91.

Melmot, S. (2008) 'Candide au Congo: l'échec annoncé de la réforme du secteur de sécurité (RSS)', Paris: Institut français des relations internationales.

MONUC (2009) 'Briefing materials: public information division, United Nations Mission in the Democratic Republic of Congo', Unpublished report.

Moyo, D. (2009) *Dead Aid: Why Aid is Not Working and How There is Another Way for Africa*, London: Allen Lane.

Mpinga, H. (1970) 'L'administration publique Congolaise: l'impact du milieu socio-politique sur sa structure et son fonctionnement', Unpublished PhD thesis, Lovanium University.

Mukoka Nsenda (1986) 'La réforme de l'administration publique au Zaïre. Quelle réforme pour quelle administration?', *Cahiers africains d'administration publique*, 27: 99–115.

Mushobekwa, E. (2009) 'Democratic Republic of Congo, Spring 2009 economic report', Kinshasa: World Bank.

Muzong W. Kodi (2007) *Anti-Corruption Challenges in Post-election Democratic Republic of Congo*, London: Chatham House.

Nzeza, A. (2004) 'The Kinshasa "bargain"', in T. Trefon (ed.), *Reinventing Order in the Congo: How People Respond to State Failure in Kinshasa*, London: Zed Books.

OECD (2008) 'Concepts and dilemmas of state building in fragile situations: from fragility to resilience', *Journal of Development*, 8(3): 1–82.

Olivier de Sardan, J.-P. (2008) 'Researching the practical norms of real governance in Africa', Discussion paper no. 5, London: Africa Power and Politics Programme/Overseas Development Institute.

Pei, M. (2007) 'Corruption threatens China's future', Policy brief no. 55, Carnegie Endowment for International Peace.

Pouligny, B. (2006) *Peace Operations Seen from Below: UN Missions and Local People*, London: Hurst.

Pourtier, R. (1997) 'Du Zaïre au Congo: un territoire en quête d'Etat', *Afrique contemporaine*, 183: 7–30.

— (2009) 'L'Etat et le territoire: contraintes et défis de la reconstruction', in T. Trefon (ed.), *Réforme au Congo (RDC): Attentes et Désillusions*, Tervuren/Paris: Musée royal de l'Afrique centrale/L'Harmattan.

Prunier, G. (2009) *From Genocide to Continental War: The 'Congolese' Conflict and Crisis of Contemporary Africa*, London: Hurst.

Rackley, E. B. (2006) 'Democratic Republic of the Congo: undoing government by predation', *Disasters*, 30(4): 417–32.

Raeymaekers, T. (2007) 'The power of protection. Governance and transborder trade on the Congo–Ugandan border', Unpublished PhD thesis, University of Ghent.

Renton, D., D. Seddon and L. Zelig (2007) *The Congo: Plunder and Resistance*, London: Zed Books.

République démocratique du Congo (2006) 'Document stratégique de croissance et de réduction de la pauvreté', Kinshasa.

— (2010) 'Rapport national des progrès des OMD', Kinshasa.

République démocratique du Congo/Assemblée nationale (2005) 'Rapport de la commission spéciale chargée de l'examen de la validité des conventions à caractère économique et financier conclues pendant les guerres de 1996–1997 et de 1998', Kinshasa.

Reyntjens, F. (2009) *The Great African War: Congo and Regional Geopolitics, 1996–2006*, Cambridge: Cambridge University Press.

Risques Internationaux (2010) 'Congo-RDC-2010: dossier sur les risques et les opportunités', no. 139, Paris: Nord Sud Expert.

Roda, J.-M. and K. Erdlenbruch (2003) 'Analyse des conditions de reprise économique du secteur forestier en République démocratique du Congo', Unpublished report, World Bank.

Rogeau, O. (2010) 'La joie et les larmes', *Le Vif L'Express*, 3077(53), 25 June–1 July.

Rubbers, B. (2009) *Faire Fortune en Afrique: Anthropologie des derniers colons du Katanga*, Paris: Karthala.

Saint-Martin, J.-G. (2008) 'Rapport d'évaluation finale. Projet d'appui à la réforme de l'administration publique', Unpublished report, Coopération technique belge/Group-conseil Baastel.

Schatzberg, M. (1988) *The Dialectics of Oppression in Zaire*, Bloomington and Indianapolis: Indiana University Press.

— (2001) *Political Legitimacy in Middle Africa: Father, Family, Food*, Bloomington and Indianapolis: Indiana University Press.

Scott, J. C. (1998) *Seeing Like a State: How Certain Schemes to Improve the Human Condition Have Failed*, New Haven, CT, and London: Yale University Press.

Stearns, J. K. (2007) 'Congo's peace: miracle or mirage?', *Current History*, 106(700): 202–7.

StrategiCo. (2007) *République démocratique du Congo: 2008*, Paris: L'Harmattan.

Sumata, C., T. Trefon and S. Cogels (2004) 'Images et usages de l'argent de la diaspora congolaise: les transferts comme vecteur d'entretien du quotidien à Kinshasa' in T. Trefon (ed.), *Ordre et Désordre à Kinshasa*, Tervuren/Paris: Institut africain/L'Harmattan.

Toft, M. D. (2010) 'Ending civil wars: a case for rebel victory?', *International Security*, 34(4): 7–36.

Trefon, T. (ed.) (2004) *Reinventing Order in the Congo: How People Respond to State Failure in Kinshasa*, London: Zed Books.

— (2008) 'La réforme du secteur forestier en République démocratique du Congo: défis sociaux et faiblesses institutionnelles', *Afrique contemporaine*, 227: 81–93.

— (2009) 'Public service provision in a failed state: looking beyond predation in the Democratic Republic of Congo', *Review of African Political Economy*, 36(119): 9–21.

Trefon, T. with B. Ngoy (2007) *Parcours administratifs dans un Etat en faillite: Récits de Lubumbashi (RDC)*, Tervuren/Paris: Institut africain-CEDAF/L'Harmattan.

Tull, D. (2005) *The Reconfiguration of Political Order in Africa: A Case Study of North Kivu (DR Congo)*, Hamburg: African Studies Institute.

Turner, T. (2007) *The Congo Wars: Conflict, Myth and Reality*, London/New York: Zed Books.

United Nations Panel of Inquiry (2003) 'Report of the panel of experts on the illegal exploitation of natural resources and other forms of wealth of the Democratic Republic of the Congo', New York: United Nations.

— (2009) 'Final report of the panel of experts on the illegal exploitation of natural resources and other forms of wealth of the Democratic Republic of the Congo', New York: United Nations.

Verheijen, T. (2008) 'Décentralisation en République démocratique du Congo: occasions et risques', Report no. 41776-ZR, Banque mondiale/Commission européenne.

Verheijen, T. and J. Mabi Mulumba (2008) 'Democratic Republic of Congo: rebuilding the public service wage system', Report no. 42515-ZR, World Bank.

Verhelst, T. with W. Tyndale (2002) 'Cultures, spirituality and development', in D. Eade, *Development and Culture*, London: Oxfam GB.

Vircoulon, T. (2009a) 'Réformer le "peace making" en République Démocratique du Congo: quand les processus de paix deviennent des systèmes d'action internationaux', Paris: Institut français des relations internationales.

— (2009b) 'Réforme de la justice: réalisations, limites et questionnements', in T. Trefon (ed.), *Réforme au Congo (RDC): Attentes et Désillusions*, Tervuren/Paris: Musée royal de l'Afrique centrale/L'Harmattan.

— (2010) *Les Coulisses de l'Aide*

Internationale en République Démocratique du Congo, Paris: L'Harmattan.

Wallis, W. (2010) 'Africa: treasure amid turmoil', *Financial Times*, 15 December.

Weiss, H. and T. Carayannis (2004) 'Reconstructing the Congo', *Journal of International Affairs*, 58(1): 115–41.

Weiss, H. and G. Nzongola-Ntalalaja (2009) 'Decentralization and the DRC: an overview', Issue paper no. 1: 'Decentralization and governance', New York: Center on International Cooperation.

White, B. W. (2004) 'The elusive *lupemba*: rumours about fame and (mis)fortune in Kinshasa', in T. Trefon (ed.), *Reinventing Order in the Congo: How People Respond to State Failure in Kinshasa*, London: Zed Books.

Willame, J.-C. (1992) *L'Automne d'un Despotisme: Pouvoir, argent et obéissance dans le Zaïre des années quatre-vingt*, Paris: Karthala.

— (2002) *L'Accord de Lusaka: Chronique d'une négociation internationale*, Tervuren/Paris: Institut africain-CEDAF/L'Harmattan.

— (2010) *La Guerre du Kivu: Vues de la salle climatisée et de la véranda*, Brussels: GRIP.

World Bank (2005) 'Democratic Republic of Congo. Economic and sector work. Governance and service delivery', Unpublished report.

Yoka, L. M. (2009) 'Kinshasa: bien-

être et développement? Bien-
être ou développement?', in T.
Trefon (ed.), *Réforme au Congo
(RDC): Attentes et Désillusions,*
Tervuren/Paris: Musée royal de
l'Afrique centrale/L'Harmattan.
Young, C. and T. Turner (1985) *The
Rise and Decline of the Zairian
State*, Madison: University of
Wisconsin Press.
Zacharie, A. (2009) 'De la dette au
développement: un chemin
semé d'embûches', in T. Trefon
(ed.), *Réforme au Congo
(RDC): Attentes et Désillusions*,
Tervuren/Paris: Musée royal de
l'Afrique centrale/L'Harmattan.
Zartman, I. W. (ed.) (1995) *Col-
lapsed States: The Disintegration
and Restoration of Legitimate
Authority*, Boulder, CO: Lynne
Rienner.
Zeebroek, X. (2009) 'La mission
des Nations Unies au Congo:
le léviathan du maintien de la
paix', in T. Trefon (ed.), *Réforme
au Congo (RDC): Attentes
et Désillusions*, Tervuren/
Paris: Musée royal de l'Afrique
centrale/L'Harmattan.

Index

About Zed Books

Zed Books is a critical and dynamic publisher, committed to increasing awareness of important international issues and to promoting diversity, alternative voices and progressive social change. We publish on politics, development, gender, the environment and economics for a global audience of students, academics, activists and general readers. Run as a co-operative, Zed Books aims to operate in an ethical and environmentally sustainable way.

Find out more at:

www.zedbooks.co.uk

For up-to-date news, articles, reviews and events information visit:

http://zed-books.blogspot.com

To subscribe to the monthly Zed Books e-newsletter, send an email headed 'subscribe' to:

marketing@zedbooks.net

We can also be found on **Facebook**, **ZNet**, **Twitter** and **Library Thing**.